Vedran Dedić

WANDERER'S JOURNEY

*A Refugee's Search for
A Home in The Beautiful Game*

Edited by: Sarah Dedić

Disclaimer:

The events herein are presented to the best of the author's memory. As we know, human memory is imperfect. Exact conversations with people or descriptions of details or events were written to the best of the author's abilities. Some people have been combined into one. A few names and identifying details have been changed for privacy reasons. The goal is to recreate the spirit of what was said, seen, or done to evoke its meaning and feeling. The stories are true with some embellishment for literary effect.

To my family

Table of Contents

Introduction: Time vii

Chapter 1: Origins 1

Chapter 2: A New Beginning 9

Chapter 3: The Five Firsts in Football 17

Chapter 4: Restart 36

Chapter 5: Closure 47

Chapter 6: Lost in the Wilderness 58

Chapter 7: Out of the Darkness, Into the Light 88

Chapter 8: On My Own..115

Chapter 9: Despair 125

Chapter 10: Hometown Heroes..150

Chapter 11: There and Back Again 176

Chapter 12: Reignited Passion 206

Chapter 13: Cosmic Justice 240

Chapter 14: La Pulga..256

Chapter 15: El Último Diez..263

Conclusion: The Final Introspection 274

Acknowledgement: Thank You...279

INTRODUCTION

Time

Football. The great sport that consists of a round ball and twenty-two players on the pitch. Football. The game that brings a community together. Football. Where said community is represented by the club on the pitch, where the supporters see themselves as part of the club and as the 12th man. Football. Where supporters dedicate hours upon hours of their time to the club. A win for the club is a win for the community and the individual supporter. Football has always provided me with beauty, joy, heartbreak, despair, and hope. All human emotions rolled into a single package. I have always loved it even during those years when I was a lapsed fan. I have always wanted to write a book about football and dabbled in unpublished and published writing about it. It was not until after Juan Román Riquelme's testimonial match, that my significant other said to me while I was again mulling about writing that "If you're going to be a writer, then write." That remark and, as the testimonial showed, that time waits for no-one, finally gave me the jolt to my system that I needed to sit down and write this book. If I was going to do what I wanted to do, it had to be now.

I wanted to write about something that would express my love for football in the context of my life's events. This includes how I grew to love the sport, how it has provided refuge mentally and emotionally, how it connected me to a community, the joy, and the psychological need for external validation. This begins with how I left the country of my birth Bosnia & Herzegovina, seeking shelter in Germany, and first falling in football-love with Borussia Dortmund. It continues with my move to the United States, losing interest in the sport due to its lack of availability, and getting roped back into it vis-à-vis Zlatan Ibrahimović's magic at Inter Milan, using football as a psychological crutch, and then reigniting the passion that I had for it as a child by discovering Boca Juniors. I hope that in this book you see some of your own life story and find a connection in it. If the spark for football has been gone from your life, I hope that this will reignite it.

CHAPTER 1

Origins

Born To Run

I was born in Bosnia & Herzegovina while it was still part of Yugoslavia. Yugoslavia had consisted of six republics which were Bosnia & Herzegovina, Croatia, Slovenia, Serbia, Montenegro, and Macedonia. It also had two autonomous provinces that were Kosovo and Vojvodina.1 The three main religions were Islam, which most Bosnians identified with; Catholicism, which most Croatians identified with; and Eastern Orthodoxy, which most Serbs identified with. Although the nomenclature is not entirely accurate, if someone identified as a Croatian living in Bosnia, it would mean most likely that they were a Bosnian Catholic who had perhaps Croatian ancestry. If someone identified as a Serb living in Bosnia, it most likely meant they were a Bosnian who practiced the Eastern Orthodox religion with Serbian ancestry. Lastly, if someone identified as Bosnian or Bosnia, they were most likely a Bosnian Muslim.

---

[1] My discussion will be limited to Bosnia & Herzegovina, Croatia, and Serbia.

Mixing an ethnicity or nationality with religion is the measure of identification in Bosnia. Josip Broz Tito, the dictator of Yugoslavia, kept all the ethnic groups and their religions controlled under the banner of unity and brotherhood, which football-wise produced very good results. Yugoslavia had finished fourth-place twice at World Cups: once at the inaugural in 1930 (pre-Tito and pre-World War II) in Uruguay and the other time in 1962 when it was hosted by Chile. In the UEFA European Championships, Yugoslavia finished runner up in 1960 and 1968 and finished fourth place in 1976. Its Olympic record is also quite respectable: winning the gold medal in 1960, the silver on three occasions in 1948, 1952, and 1956, and the bronze in 1984. At its last World Cup appearance in 1990, before the civil war started, the team was dubbed "the Brazilians of Europe" due to their style of play and the talented and stylish players in the squad which included Safet Sušić, Darko Pančev, Dragan Stojković, Robert Prosinečki, and countless others who already had or were going to have successful careers at the top clubs in Europe. They would take Maradona's Argentina all the way to penalties in the quarter-final with 10 men, only to lose 3-2 after Sergio Goycochea saved the last two penalties.

After Tito's death in May 1980, nationalist sentiments arose which started independence movements. My appearance in the world occurred when the pot was simmering due to the ethnic issues between the Serbs, Croats, and Bosnians. This tension was not only limited to Bosnia geographically, but it also spilled into Croatia and Serbia.

For my family and I, we lived comfortably in the Mejdan neighborhood of Banja Luka, a city located in northwest Bosnia and the country's second biggest city after the capital Sarajevo. My parents' marriage is what they called a mixed-marriage in Yugoslavia. My mother was of Croatian origin – ethnically speaking (although she lived in Bosnia since she was a child) and my father was Bosnian. We lived in a decent flat of a huge building that was surrounded by others that played to the Brutalist architecture of the communist times. My father's family had lived in Banja Luka for roughly three-hundred years. My paternal grandfather was initially a brick mason before being a maintenance man for a local newspaper. Now my mother's family was originally from the Slavonia region in Croatia. Her parents moved to Banja Luka and were landlords. Sadly, my mother's father died when she was nine years old from cancer. Her mother later remarried.

My father was a payroll administrator at the local hospital. My mother was a saleswoman at a department store in the city center. My father's parents lived a walk-able distance from us in a neighborhood called Potok, where my father grew up. It was rather a rough area, but my father was the first one to finish college in the neighborhood. The joke in the neighborhood was that a statue would be erected for him because of his accomplishment. My mother's mother and step-father lived in an area called Paprikovac, northwest of downtown Banja Luka, farther away from us, but still a walk-able distance as well. My grandparents would watch me while my parents worked. We were a tight-knit family. Things were good for us from the faint memories I can muster, the home videos that were preserved, and stories that had been told to me.

Unfortunately, our little paradise was being lost. The drums of war began to pound. April 6, 1992, has been given as the official date of the start of the war in Bosnia. In football myth, the kickoff to the war in Croatia started on May 13, 1990, when Dinamo Zagreb, at home, played Red Star Belgrade. Both clubs were arguably the top two biggest teams in Yugoslavia, but with brewing nationalist sentiments, tensions were even higher than normal. The two ultra groups of the respective teams clashed, and a riot ensued. Dinamo's Bad Blue Boys against Red Star's Delije. During the chaos, a policeman (who was Bosniak) was mistreating a Dinamo supporter. One of Dinamo's players and stars, Zvonimir Boban kicked the policeman in the face. The Bad Blue Boys formed a human shield around Boban to protect him. By his reaction against the policeman, an icon for Croatian independence was born.

Although the powder keg had been lit, the Yugoslav league did not dissolve immediately, nor did Bosnian players or Croatian players abandon Serbian teams and vice versa. This would prove to be one last hurrah for everyone involved. Red Star Belgrade managed to get itself to the final of the European Cup, the predecessor to the UEFA Champions League. They beat Bayern München in a hotly contested semi-final. They would play Olympique Marseille in the final. Both teams fielded great players. Red Star had Robert Prosinečki, Siniša Mihajlović, Darko Pančev, and Dejan Savićević, who all would leave the following season or two to join European heavyweight clubs. Marseille's squad included Abedi Pele, Jean-Pierre Papin, and Chris Waddle. This was supposed to be a football spectacle. However, it turned out to be a very drab final. Red Star, despite playing scintillating football in previous rounds of the competition as well as in their domestic league, chose to play the match very defensively, robbing the spectators of an entertaining final. The match went to penalty kicks, which Red Star won. It turned out to be Red Star Belgrade's only European Cup up to date. They would go on to play in the Intercontinental Cup against Colo-Colo from Chile, who were the winners of South America's premier club competition, the

Copa Libertadores. They would handily beat Colo-Colo 3-0. Despite the nationalist sentiments springing up and becoming the political zeitgeist, football was still successful with different nationalities and ethnicities playing their part in its success.

The war would also affect the national team's future. Yugoslavia qualified for the Euros in 1992 with top players from all the Yugoslav nations, finishing top of their qualifying group. However, due to the outbreak of war, they were banned by UN sanctions. The golden generation that played at the World Cup in 1990 with an addition of a few fresher legs was not meant to have another shot at glory. Yugoslavian football, on the national scale, died not with a bang, but with a whimper. Of course, I did not get to witness any of this as I was a toddler.

With the war underway, what were my parents and I going to do? Well, as luck and perhaps divine intervention would have it, we had a relative-in-law who was a guest worker in Germany for over a decade that sent us a visa. This was my mother's stepdad's brother. We left Banja Luka in October 1992, leaving all the grandparents behind. Everything that we had done and built was left in the rearview mirror. It was difficult emotionally. Was I ever going to see my grandparents again? Were my parents ever going to see *their* parents again? God only knew. We were not the only ones who had to leave our home behind. My paternal grandparents were also nomads during the war. When we left, they began living in our flat as it was deemed safer than Potok. After living there for a couple of months, the Serbian military kicked them out and gave the flat to another Serb family. They had to return to Potok where they lived until August 1995 while the war raged on around them. On my mother's side, things were somewhat better in terms of protection from the war. My maternal grandmother was married to an ethnic Serb so she was left alone. During the war, my maternal grandmother would remain in Banja Luka. She would not have to relocate and be displaced due to her husband's ethnic status.

During our sojourn to Germany, we had to stop in Zagreb on the way because the visa process had to be concluded there. Our stay lasted about a week. We stayed with my dad's cousin the entirety of our stop in Zagreb. They had a parrot that terrified me when it was let loose to fly in the flat. The opposing military forces were night-time boogeymen; that parrot was the real danger to me! During our stay, we made a day trip to visit one of my mother's uncles, who had not met me or my father, in a town outside of Zagreb. While on the train, we were unfortunately pickpocketed and lost a significant amount of money. This was money for the transportation to Germany. Due to sheer luck or divine intervention, my mother's uncle gave us half of what we lost (this was a gift to me as he had never met me). On top of that, my parents had a friend, who had a friend that loaned us the other half, which we were instructed to repay to her mother, who lived in Banja Luka. The money was repaid a short while later through my grandparents. We finally had the money to go to Germany. Besides the pickpocketing incident, we were lucky that on the way to Croatia and to Germany, no military forces bothered us. One of the few vivid memories I recall was getting off the bus in Germany once we reached our final destination, Mülheim an der Ruhr. Mülheim was in the heart of West Germany and the Ruhr Area in the state of Nordrhein-Westfalen. In the early morning, with the autumn sun beaming down on the concrete, we got off the bus. The street seemed incredibly wide, pavement all around with no traffic strangely enough. It seemed like we were dropped off on another planet.

CHAPTER 2

A New Beginning

Wind of Change

The country of Germany reunified in 1990 after decades of being divided as West Germany and East Germany. With Yugoslavia in the process of breaking up and Germany putting itself together again, we hoped that our new home would offer more opportunity, stability, and perhaps permanency. Post World War II, the Ruhr region's economy was built on coal and steel. This created a large working class who would spend their leisure time on football. Clubs like Borussia Dortmund and Schalke 04 were working-class clubs and would center their identities around that ethos. It also meant that Germany needed workers so immigrants and refugees from places like Yugoslavia and Türkiye were plentiful in this area.

Our hosts were my mother's step-uncle, his wife, adult son, the son's wife, and their small children. The step-uncle's family were guest-workers in Germany but had lived there since the early 1980s. We would stay with them for several months before German immigration authorities helped us to be placed in an unused school that was converted as a home for refugee families in a part of Mülheim called Mintard. Each family had their own room, so to speak. The kitchen and bathrooms were communal. You would have to use a dresser or an armoire to create separation within the room itself. I would start kindergarten soon thereafter while my mother was a laundromat worker/maid and my father worked in landscaping. It was in kindergarten that I first remember kicking a football with the German kids. At the time, I don't remember feeling looked at like an outsider by the Germans. We were just small kids. But that perception would change later.

Our situation would improve little by little over the years. Of course, there was always the dread that our visa would not be extended after every six months or that the grandparents back in Bosnia would be displaced somewhere. But all we could do is hope and pray for the best and continue living our lives. Constant worry and despair could not take over. We needed cautious optimism to keep our sanity. This would be tested several times but especially in August 1995. While the war was still going on, we lost contact for several days with my paternal grandparents. The worst thoughts were brewing in our heads. Where were they? Were they dead? The worry during those few days was palpable. My mother reached out to her relatives in Bosnia and Croatia to see if they could help find any information. I remember her once running back to our room from the payphone in the refugee camp crying because there was no news. Ultimately, contact was established. They became displaced people themselves being housed on a Croatian island named Obonjan. They even made the evening news being shown on boats. It was like a ton of bricks had been taken off our shoulders. They were alive and safe and that was the most important thing. They would stay in Croatia for a couple of years before relocating to a town called Sanski Most where one of our relatives had property there. Throughout their displacement, we would always send them some of our hard-earned money to make their lives a bit more bearable in their temporary environment.

During the early part of our stay, while the grandparents were waiting the war out in Potok, we added a member to our family; I became a big brother to my newborn sister. After her birth, we moved to a different part of Mülheim. This was another refugee camp. The most apt description would be like an American trailer home but much longer. We dubbed it "The Container." Again, each family would have their room but each room this time had smaller rooms within it which were divided by walls. This was enough space for my parents, my newborn sister, and me. Behind The Container was a *spielplatz* or playground for children. We used a fence that neighbored the other side (which were apartments/condos where Germans overwhelmingly resided) and the back of our own building as our "goals" when we played football. This was the sacred ground where I learned to play the beautiful game. There were five other boys around my age and the *spielplatz* would become a football pitch. There were Memo and Denis, both from the Bosnian capital Sarajevo, Ado from Gornji Agići, Sano from a village near Bihać, and Billy from Dubica, who got that nickname because when we played Power Rangers on the playground, he would be the blue one. We were nicknamed "Mali Šarafi" which literally translated to "little bolts" or "little screws." My father would be the ref and we would play 3 vs 3. On days that my mother was working, we would beg other ladies in The Container to watch my little sister so my father could ref our games. After refereeing several matches, my father would get tired of it, so we had to beg him to continue. We would occasionally walk out before the matches hand in hand à la the Brazilians in the mid to late 1990s. Football fervor just kind of happened to all of us as we were growing up. I preferred playing as a striker at that age, as they were the ones who scored the goals and got all the glory. Sometimes when no one could watch my sister, my dad and I would play football with her in our home. He would lob the little red-and-black ball to her, and she would kick the ball while I would play goalkeeper in the doorway.

At this stage, I started elementary school. The Germans call this *Grundschule*. The elementary-aged kids in the refugee camp would make the short five-to-ten-minute walk to attend school, usually with an adult accompanying us on our way. Although we knew we were different from the Germans, there was not a huge animosity amongst the children. Football became the universal language between non-Germans and Germans in general. I was the only male refugee in my specific class and had no problems with my classmates. We would play football in the school yard every recess that we could. It would be the highlight of school for me. Playing football with the Germans was a good way of harmonizing relations with our hosts. Hasan, who was from Türkiye and had a playing style of Bulgarian playmaker Krasimir Balakov, was the other non-German in the class and he made an excellent partner on the pitch. We would emulate our football heroes that we would see on TV. For me, I loved Ronaldo (who everyone else adored as well), another Brazilian named Giovane Élber who plied his trade at Bundesliga club VfB Stuttgart and later Bayern München, Andreas "Andy" Möller who was Borussia Dortmund's playmaker, and goal-getter Ulf Kirsten from Bayer Leverkusen. If you asked kids at the time who they thought was the best, chances were high that they would say Ronaldo. His dribbling at a rapid pace, his ball control, ability to get out of tight spots, and goal-scoring prowess left everyone in awe. He would do it in such a style and with such flair that he seemed unstoppable. He was the torch bearer for the famous *jogo bonito* from Brazil for my generation. Because of him, the imagery that was conjured up out of my mind of Brazil was his countrymen playing this style of football on Copacabana Beach with "Samba de Janeiro" by Bellini or "Mas Que Nada" by Sergio Mendes playing in the background. Ronaldo was my first football idol and was the ideal Brazilian footballer for me. His style would always be something that I looked for in future players and teams.

Besides playing in the school yard or back at the refugee camp, football would permeate my life in other ways. I would buy football magazines and play football games like EA Sports's *FIFA: Road to World Cup 98* on the original PlayStation with my buddy Denis. In addition, football stickers by Panini were the big thing. You would purchase an empty album and collect stickers to complete it. Any duplicates that you would have, you would trade with friends and schoolmates. We would stop outside of school in a little kiosk where we would buy these items on a regular basis. First, it was for the Bundesliga, and then the World Cup in 1998. However, I never completed any of these albums at the time. Afternoons would be spent watching *Captain Tsubasa*, a coming-of-age anime from Japan that focused on the titular character's friendships, rivalries, and football matches.

    Lastly, football was an opportunity to bond with my dad. Every Saturday evening, a TV program called *Ran Fußball* would show the highlights of that Bundesliga's match day. We would discuss goals and plays. An overwhelming majority of Bundesliga matches were available only behind a sports package. With our limited income at the time, *Ran Fußball* would have to do. We would also regularly check the match scores on our neighbor's television through teletext. On Sunday nights, there was a different TV program that would show highlights from other European countries including Italy's Serie A and Spain's La Liga. This is where I would be exposed to Robert Baggio, Alessandro Del Piero, Gabriel Batistuta, Raúl, Luis Enrique, Rivaldo, and of course Ronaldo. Luckily our football was not limited to watching highlight shows; continental competitions such as the UEFA Champions' League would be shown on public television as well as international matches between national teams, whether friendly or not. My preference for national team competitions over club competitions is borne out of nostalgia, since the first match I remember as being truly exceptional was played by the German national team, as well as my greater familiarity with the national squads due to regularly having access to international matches. Of course, there was also something special about putting on the shirt of your country and representing it to the best of your talents. In Germany, we were all former Yugoslavs. The separators, like what region or city you came from, were secondary. My preference, in hindsight, made perfect sense.

CHAPTER 3

The Five Firsts in Football

Leaving on a Jet Plane

First Match:

It was a warm summer in Mülheim. I had just finished first grade with very good marks. Our living situation remained the same. We had been in Germany for nearly four years now. The war in Bosnia had officially ended with the Dayton Peace Agreement in December 1995. We were still unsure where our future lay. Were the Germans going to kick us out and send us back to Bosnia in its post-war state? I had no idea. My parents shielded me from the uncertainty and stress we were going through. This meant I could basically just focus on school and my hobbies.

Euro '96 took place in the month of June. England vs. Germany in the semi-finals is the first match I recall watching on the small television in our kitchen. I remember the massive size of Wembley Stadium. The Germans wore beautiful white kits, sponsored by Adidas, and the English wore gray-blue kits sponsored by Umbro. My dad sat in his recliner while I sat on the floor to his left. I remember Paul Gascoigne, Alan Shearer, and David Seaman. Those were the English players that stood out to me. On the German side, I remember Andreas Möller, Germany's playmaker and Andreas Köpke, the goalkeeper. The match came down to penalties. English defender (and future England manager) Gareth Southgate took England's sixth penalty. He went low but also too close to the center of the goal. Köpke guessed correctly and saved it. Möller took Germany's sixth penalty. If Möller scored, Germany would be through to the final without him as he had accumulated too many yellows. A powerful shot down the top middle of the goal and Seaman moving to his right sent Germany to the final. Möller celebrated his goal as Paul Gascoigne had done with his chin up and arms on his hips previously but in mockery and pride of beating the English on home soil in their cathedral of a stadium. I was happy for my host country to progress to the final and this was my first taste of what international football was about. To me, it appeared that it was a big deal for one country to beat another. Even to this day, I place international tournaments like the World Cup and Copa America over club tournaments like the Copa Libertadores and the Champions League. While club football has lost some of its charm due to its overcommercialization, international football still retains some of its romance -- glory for your soil, your country, and your culture.

First Football Love

You don't forget the first football club you fell in love with. For me, it started at elementary school in Germany. *Die Grundschule an der Saarner Straße* in Mülheim an der Ruhr. I sat next to the only left-handed kid in the class, Maurice. Left-handedness was at the time strange to me, like a deformity, since everyone else in the classroom was right-handed. The teacher, Frau Seggelke, seated us next to each other. I naturally had to sit next to Maurice's right side so our arms wouldn't get in each other's way when we were writing assignments. One day we got to chatting about football. He mentioned that he liked Borussia Dortmund especially their players Andreas "Andy" Möller and Lars Ricken. This piqued my interest, and I began to follow Dortmund as much as I could considering on-demand Bundesliga games were behind a paywall. This meant that 99% of the time I had to settle for *Ran Fußball* at 18:00 on Saturday. My dad and I would watch this religiously, as it was our weekly football fix along with the occasional game on public TV. However, Champions League matches were midweek and on public TV and this is where I experienced the feeling of those famous European nights.

Dortmund qualified for the Champions League in 1996-1997 by virtue of winning the Bundesliga in 1995-1996. They would play teams that I was exposed to for the first time like Manchester United and Juventus. The mystery and awe that surrounded these teams was palpable. Football had not been fully globalized yet. Wide access to the internet was not available and certainly there was no streaming yet. A chance to see foreign teams and players on a regular basis would be available on highlight shows or one would read about them in specialty magazines or newspapers. In this way, you would sort of figure out who the important players on the team were that you should pay attention to. Sitting on the living room floor, I stared in amazement at the TV. To my child eyes, watching Dortmund take on Manchester United was the height of drama, on par with the great Shakespearean tragedies. One figure from the opposing team stood out, a man over six feet tall with his collar popped. This was Eric Cantona. The way he moved about the pitch, his elegance, drive, and determination made an impression on me. It was a player I would not forget. Dortmund would beat Manchester United 1-0 at the Westfalenstadion thanks to a bullet outside of the box by René Tretschok. The return leg at Old Trafford would decide this tie. In the 8th minute, playmaker Andy Möller found starlet Lars Ricken in the box, who turned around and sent a low but powerful shot past legendary Peter Schmeichel into the keeper's bottom right corner. Dortmund were leading 2-0 on aggregate now. Later in the match, Manchester United had more possession of the ball but a key block by Jürgen Kohler from a potential Cantona tap-in kept the score 1-0. United would continue to attack and create chances and shots on goal but Dortmund's defense remained resolute, and the match finished 0-1 in favor of the visitors. Borussia Dortmund was heading to their first European Cup/Champions League final. Their opposition would be Juventus from Italy.

On May 28, 1997, Dortmund would face Juventus at the Olympiastadion in München. I remember it being a warm night in May without the humidity that I would have to get accustomed to later. I recall the sun setting behind the neighboring apartment buildings and an extra burst of orange appearing on the horizon. I took my place, which was on the floor in front of the TV with my father sitting behind me in his recliner. The teams came out and the famous Champions League anthem played. The heavenly sounds gave me goosebumps and I fidgeted in impatient anticipation for kickoff. This was my first Champions League final and the team I supported was in it. Dortmund were the underdogs. Juventus had a star-studded team of Christian Vieri, Didier Deschamps, Alen Bokšić, Ciro Ferrara, and the recently acquired Zinedine

Zidane from Bordeaux and a bench that included Alessandro Del Piero. However, BVB certainly did not play like underdogs. Two goals in quick succession from Karl Heinz-Riedle in the 29th and 34th minute had BVB in the driver's seat. Zidane was marked out of the game by Scotsman Paul Lambert. Juventus looked toothless. Marcello Lippi subbed in Del Piero at half-time and Juve turned up the heat, trying to get back into the match. They would find a goal with a Del Piero back-heel in the 65th minute. Ottmar Hitzfeld had an ace up his sleeve and introduced Dortmund local boy, Lars Ricken in the 70th minute. Juve kept pushing on for an equalizer, but they lost possession and Dortmund's number ten Andy Möller played a through-ball to Ricken, who lobbed Angelo Peruzzi from about 20 yards out with his first touch of the game. Ricken had scored roughly 16 seconds after coming on. It was over. Dortmund were European Champions for the first time in their history. I was quite happy that Dortmund won, but I don't recall any other emotions coming into play. I was still just a kid. I didn't necessarily understand or appreciate the communal, psychological, emotional, and societal impact that football had at the time. It was basically that I liked this team and I hoped the opposing team would lose and if it was a classmate's team, I could make jokes at their expense.

First Jersey

While we were still living in The Container and my support for BVB had gone past its infancy, it was time to get a BVB jersey for the 1997-1998 season. My mother and I went all over town to find the newest kind. Get on the bus, get off the bus, get on the tram, get off the tram, but we could not find any. Maybe we looked in the wrong places or we did not look hard enough. At this point, due to my disappointment and frustration as a 9-year-old, I made a very irrational decision. Most likely my decision was based on peer pressure and wanting a football jersey for its own sake. I ended up purchasing an FC Bayern München jersey. I did not support Bayern, but my group of friends were Bayern fans. As a matter of fact, a small rivalry emerged between Bayern and Dortmund at that time due to Dortmund's success. And yet here I was, caving in to peer pressure, buying the jersey of the rivals. The jersey was aesthetically appealing, but I would not make the same decision now as I did back then.

First Match Experiences

My friend Nerko, his cousin Memo, and I went to my first professional football match with our dads. Our closest Bundesliga team was MSV Duisburg and they would play the other Borussia, Mönchengladbach. It was May 24, 1997. It was a very short ride to the then-existing Wedaustadion, which held a capacity of a little over 30,000. We arrived at the stadium and bought tickets in the away section, behind the goal. I walked up the steps to the stands with my father, hand-in-hand, and saw a mass of thousands and thousands of people, most dressed in Duisburg's blue and white. The opposing end appeared to be on the horizon that never ended. I do not remember much about the match except that Duisburg beat Gladbach 4-2. I did not really care which team won; it was my first football match and I soaked in the experience. What stood out was the atmosphere – it seemed that the supporters were constantly engaged with what was happening on the pitch.

We would repeat the same trip the next season and bought tickets in the away end again. This time, we watched Duisburg take on the mighty Bayern München, who were in a Bundesliga title race with newly promoted FC Kaiserslautern. FCK had been a historical German club who had success in the past but were relegated to the 2nd Bundesliga in 1996. In the 1996-1997 season, they won the 2nd Bundesliga and returned to the 1st Bundesliga. Not many people expected them to be in a title race their first season back in the topflight. However, they surpassed expectations; they were in the driver's seat and Bayern needed to beat Duisburg to push FCK to the last matchday. My experience was a little different this time due to the significance of the match. Although we were behind the goal, I was amazed to see Oliver Kahn, Lothar Matthäus, and others. These were world class players in front of me. I appreciated what was happening on the pitch a lot more than I did the previous year. Bayern and Duisburg played a nil-nil draw. Kaiserslautern was playing Wolfsburg at home and beat them 4-0. That meant that Kaiserslautern were German champions -- not only champions, but also winners of the Bundesliga in their first season back. It was a unique accomplishment. This is also the first time I saw someone suffer football heartbreak. A man with a denim jacket covered with Bayern insignia was beside himself in tears after the final whistle blew. He knew Bayern had screwed the pooch and Kaiserslautern were champions. It is an image I will not forget as I realized that football meant a lot more than kicking the ball about the pitch. This happened to be my last Bundesliga match in person for a while. Of course, I did not know at the time. I would have to wait until 2019 to step foot inside a German stadium again.

First World Cup

Unsurprising as it may sound, each World Cup evokes memories of not only the football, but also whatever else was going on in my life at the time. It's a reference point for me. The way that some people may remember pivotal life events as being "two days before my birthday" or "just after our anniversary," I tell time on the World Cup calendar.

With France 1998, I just finished the third grade and was into year six as a refugee in Deutschland. With school out and the spring fading and the summer heat slowly making its presence known, the event of the year was a few days from starting. At this point, I was allowed to travel to the city center on my own via tram to hang out. The sound of Ricky Martin's "The Cup of Life" was the theme song of the World Cup and it would be heard quite a bit in the summer in the main strip of the center where I would walk around and enjoy what my 9-year-old self thought was the most luxurious food…Mickey D's. We hardly went to any restaurants when we lived there so going out to McDonald's, together as a family or alone, was a big deal to me. McDonald's added to the World Cup fever by proudly advertising a small replica version of the official match ball. I stood in line and stared at the glossy poster, all thought of cheeseburgers forgotten, but I was heartbroken when we reached the counter only to be told that they had already sold out. I was griping to my friends at the Container that I wasn't able to get one of these balls. Thankfully my friend Memo got me one from across town. He knocked on our door at The Container and said "Hey, you're missing something," and threw the ball across the room towards me. It was a gesture of genuine friendship. The euphoria encapsulated us even further as my friends and I would collect the stickers for the World Cup album issued by Panini.

Onto the actual football. As host, France were one of the favorites with a mixture of players coming from immigrant backgrounds, most notably Zinedine Zidane. This was hyped as the New France. Of course, Brazil were also favorites with Ronaldo in phenomenal form for club and country. As to my host country, new talent wasn't coming through the ranks - Germany was depending on veteran players who had won the Euros two years prior.

The tournament did not disappoint. You would finally get the chance to see those players who had had an aura of mystery surrounding them. The commentators would praise players like Dennis Bergkamp, Raúl, and Carlos Valderrama -- players I would not see on a regular basis, but whose reputation as skillful masters of the round ball created an enigma around them and wowed me when I saw them perform. The national anthems played before each match were a battle cry roared by thousands. Supporters in the stands would wear things symbolic or traditional of the country that they supported. The image was colorful and vibrant. It was like the entire world was squeezed, downsized, and crammed into these French stadiums for one month. It felt important. It felt energetic. It felt like life itself.

The match that had the most personal meaning to me was when Germany played Croatia in the quarterfinals. This was Croatia's first appearance as an independent country at a World Cup since the breakup of Yugoslavia. Croatia had a team full of talent spread out in the top leagues of Europe. And it would show during this match because the Germans were soundly defeated, losing 3-0 to the team with the checkered kits. As mentioned earlier, the playground of our refugee camp backed up to numerous apartment buildings inhabited by Germans. While the Germans allowed us to live in their country during the war, certain small segments of the German population still viewed us as second-class residents and put their noses up at us. I knew from experience that there were quite a few of those types in those apartment buildings. While not everyone was a Croat where we lived, Croatia was basically the de facto representation for us. So when Croatia beat the Germans, it was a big "screw you, we matter and we are just as good as you" to that certain segment on the other side of the fence. The cheers at The Container were quite the contrast to the silence at the apartments. This was our victory.

Unfortunately, Croatia lost in a hotly contested semifinal against France but ended up beating the Netherlands in the third-place match. The Container was proud of Croatia for exceeding expectations and representing the former Yugoslavia so well in their maiden World Cup appearance as an independent country.

The final ended up being the two favorites: France versus Brazil. This was Zinedine Zidane vs. Ronaldo. This was a battle of the new giants of football. But fate had another plan for that day. Ronaldo mysteriously became sick on the day of the final. The rumors of whether he was going to start or even play at all made their way around the stadium and around the world. I was shocked that one of my football idols was not going to play in the final. The biggest match of the year and my football idol was sick. I hoped he was okay with whatever was happening to him. Ultimately, when the final line-ups were announced, Ronaldo was in the starting eleven. However, he understandably did not perform to his usual standard. His counterpart on the French team, Zinedine Zidane announced himself to the rest of the world and began his legend by scoring two goals in the final and leading France to their first ever World Cup title. The French deservedly won, but one has to ponder the "what if?" What if Ronaldo had not had his medical episode? How would he have fared then? How would the rest of his team have responded since the psychological effect of his illness would not have been present? These questions have been sucked into the endless black hole of football debates, to be argued repeatedly with no clear answer. The tournament was now over and it was every bit the spectacle it was hyped up to be. This World Cup set the template for all future World Cups for me.

As for me personally, by the end of that summer, I would begin 4th grade and take the bus and tram across town to attend school when before it would be just a short walk. Most importantly, our living arrangements improved and we started living in flats that were occupied by English soldiers after World War II. The rest of the apartments were also occupied by refugees from the former Yugoslavia. Unfortunately, these were not the same people that we shared the previous refugee camp with. After the war had concluded, the German government slowly started telling refugees from Yugoslavia that they needed to leave Germany. Some of those people moved back to Bosnia or Croatia. Others moved to the United States of America or Canada or Australia. As a kid, I didn't really realize that I would perhaps never see my friends in person again. Only Ado moved over with his family to these new flats. The "Mali Šarafi" went their own ways, some returning to their places of origin, while others looked for new homes.

Although we moved to a different spot in town, we could not continue doing this in perpetuity. We were continuously under stress that the visa in Germany would not be renewed. We had the opportunity to apply to come to the USA under a program for displaced individuals and families. We already knew some people that went to the States and settled in St. Louis and Atlanta. We had this application for thirteen months before we decided to apply. Thirteen months of deciding whether we were going to return to Bosnia to be with my grandparents or try to make our home in America. I am not sure what the deciding factor ended up being since I wasn't privy to the decision-making process, but we took our chance and applied to come to America. In the spring of 1999, we were granted an interview in Frankfurt. The train ride was several hours, but I saw the beautiful German countryside with its vibrant green meadows and sparkling bodies of water. We waited with dozens and dozens of other people to be interviewed in some government building and then we were called in. An interpreter was present and one or two officials and the four of us. The interview was over within minutes, and we were told to get examined by medical staff at some other location. After doing so, we returned to Mülheim by train again that evening. Now the waiting game began. We were waiting to hear if we would go to the States, hoping that we could make our home on American soil and have a bit more certainty in our future.

Around the same time while we were waiting on an answer regarding our application to the States, the German government sent us a letter, telling us that we had to leave the country by a certain date. With no answer on the application to come to the States, worry set in. However, that worry was short-lived. We received an answer from the United States government. Their answer came much sooner than anyone of us expected. In mid-to-late July, we received word that we would be traveling to the US on August 20, 1999 to a place called Mobile, Alabama. Initially, we requested a town in Michigan because my dad had a friend there, but since he was not family and we did not have any family in the States, the immigration authorities sent us to Mobile. We had never heard of this city. We found it on the map and someone in Germany, who had access to the internet when it was not that common, informed us that the rapper Tupac was from Mobile (of course that turned out to be completely false as I found out later on). My exposure to America was through TV: *Baywatch*, *Buffy the Vampire Slayer*, *Everybody Loves Raymond*, and the various 80s action films. My father and I would get up at 3 AM local time to watch Michael Jordan and the Chicago Bulls play the Utah Jazz in the NBA Finals. I thought of palm trees, skyscrapers, and tenements with fire escapes. That's what America was to my ten-year-old mind. We were excited and thrilled, but also of course nervous since we would have to restart our lives again in another country across the Atlantic Ocean. We were already far away from any family in Bosnia – this created an even bigger distance. School-wise, I finished fourth grade in June and was one of the two kids from my class to go to gymnasium, the highest tier of upper school in Germany. After receiving word of our move, I went to gymnasium for a few weeks just to see what it was like. August 20 came quickly. We woke up in the early morning hours and were picked up by two men in a white van. They provided the transport and took us to Frankfurt airport, which was roughly a three-hour ride from Mülheim. After arriving at the airport, we had breakfast at McDonald's, which looking back on it seemed the most appropriate thing to do. McDonald's was an advertisement for the United States of America, a taste of what was to come.

Our itinerary was Frankfurt → New York City (JFK Airport) → Atlanta → Mobile. There were many other Balkan travelers on the plane, all going to their new home. This was my first time on a plane, and I had a window seat. I read about the Bermuda triangle where planes and ships would disappear, but my ten-year-old nerves were calmed when my father told me that we were not going that route, probably much to his amusement. The flight to JFK was going to take about 7 hours or so. When we were preparing to land at JFK, I caught a glimpse of the Statue of Liberty out of my window and so did the kid in front of me. We turned to each other in amazement. It was a welcome sign. Unfortunately, I did not have a dramatic music score playing in the background to add to the gravity and emotion of the moment.

At JFK, we received our immigration papers and caught our flight to Atlanta. We had help through this process by interpreters. However, arriving in Atlanta, we did not and that's when my anxiety ramped up. I began to imagine doomsday scenarios over and over again. What if we got on the wrong plane? What if we couldn't understand the signs in the airport? What if we could not communicate with the airport staff? My dad took evening English classes in Germany, but what if he did not know a word? Luckily, he did not need to know much, as Atlanta airport staff were clear in their instructions. This fear of not being able to communicate was a repeating theme which would carry on throughout the beginning of our lives in the US. You do not want to look like an idiot, or worse, get lost and be left behind. We sat on the tarmac for over an hour due to bad weather, but finally took off. Mobile was only an hour away via plane, so it was a short flight. We could not wait to get to our new destination. This trip dragged on forever.

At the Mobile airport, two representatives of Catholic Social Services awaited us. They were the welcoming committee, and they were also from the former Yugoslavia. Once we grabbed our luggage and exited the small airport, the first indicator of our new home was the malevolent August heat. It was as if someone put us in a really, really hot oven. It was hotter than Hades. After getting our first feel of our new surroundings, the air conditioner in the car cooled us off and made us realize that unlike in Europe, air conditioning is essential to combat the heat and to even live in the American South. The airport was about 25 minutes from our apartment. Driving down the main strip on a Friday night, we passed endless bright, neon lights. It was America like I had seen in movies.

Our apartment was on the top floor of a two-story duplex surrounded by other duplexes. We dragged our luggage up the wooden stairs. There was a living room, two bedrooms, a bathroom, and a kitchen. A couch was already there along with some mattresses for sleeping and a kitchen table. No actual beds yet, no TV, no dressers. We were exhausted from our long trip. Before we went to sleep, my little sister, asked with naïveté, "when are we going home?"

CHAPTER 4

Restart

American Land

When I woke up the day after our arrival, reality sunk in. I felt like as if I was just born again. A clean slate, a *tabula rasa*. It was the same feeling when we made it to Germany: as if we were on another planet. Within two weeks of our arrival, Catholic Social Services set up my father at a door production company. My mother was initially employed as a hotel maid and then shortly after at a commercial laundromat. My sister started preschool. Mobile had a small-sized community from the former Yugoslavia which would balloon up to around 300 people. What struck me initially was the lack of reliable public transport in Mobile. If you didn't have a car, your options were to walk, wait on a bus that may or may not come, or get your neighbor to take you wherever you needed to go. Although we met some Bosnian folks within a few days of coming to the States, we couldn't impose on them to take us everywhere we needed to go. Case in point, one day my father and I walked to a supermarket called Delchamps in the sweltering August sun. The walk was about twenty minutes there and even longer walking back laden with the week's groceries; the temperature made it seem an eternity. Living without a car was just difficult, if not impossible. Another culture shock to me was basic food items. The bread that we bought tasted different than any of the bread I was used to in Germany – it didn't feel very filling and sometimes would stick to your teeth and the roof of your mouth. Luckily, later, we used the power of Bosnian gossip to find better bread at an actual bakery. The food at the supermarket tasted differently than I was accustomed to and it took a little while for us to get used to. What about leisure activities? We were limited in the beginning as to what we could do with lack of transportation, the summer heat, and not settling in yet. So we bought a TV. For the first few months, we didn't have cable. Just the local channels. One Saturday morning, after we bought our first TV, Eddie Murphy's *Coming to America* was on. It was our first film in the States. What are the odds, right?

My American education began with middle school. There were a few other former Yugoslavia kids who lived in the same apartments as we did who also attended the school. The first day of school was the Friday before Labor Day for me. I walked to the bus stop with the Yugos. The big yellow bus pulled up, like

I had seen in American cinema before. This was the first time I heard English spoken in very close quarters. You are more self-conscious of a foreign language when you are older. I did not get the same feeling when I started kindergarten in Germany. The looks of curiosity from the Americans – like I was some wild exotic animal – were piercing. The fact that we had to wear school uniforms also seemed odd to me; in Germany, we could wear whatever we wanted. Lunch was served in the cafeteria by workers that were referred to as the "lunch ladies." One would line up in a queue, grab a tray, and select something out of two or three entrée choices on the menu for the day. I got past that part with no problem since I could point to what I wanted, but once I got to the register to pay, the first memorable language barrier occurred for me. We were told the school would provide free lunch. Bad information led to a situation where I, in broken English and a strong accent, uttered the words "no money" to the woman who was taking payment. After a moment of embarrassment and awkwardness, while a line of hungry students stood impatiently waiting behind me, she waived me through without having to pay. It turned out that some of the paperwork for this part had not been completed. Once it was, a number was provided to me, and every day I would tell it to the woman at the register to receive my lunch for free. This assistance was provided through the government. Eventually the lunch at school would cease being free but still quite cheap even at full price of $1.75 or reduced price of 75¢. In addition, my family received some sort of government assistance for a few months after arriving until we found our feet. That soon stopped too. Fortunately, we were able to buy a car within a few months, so we didn't have to rely on neighbors or Catholic Social Services for transport. Coincidentally enough, one of my father's American coworkers gave him a cassette tape, our first one for the new car, of the Southern rock band, Lynyrd Skynyrd. The first song on the tape? "Sweet Home Alabama."

About two weeks after starting school, my English language skills would be tested. One of my teachers made me stand in front of the class to introduce myself and to see how much English I had learned. It was the first real challenge for me in the US. I stood up there, with broken English, saying biographical details about myself and my family. At times, when I would struggle to say something, anything, whether content wise or trying to figure out a way to say it in English, I would hang my head and think real hard while the eyes of classmates would burn into me and a suffocating silence came over the classroom, waiting on my next words. The challenge, the pressure, the anxiety and discomfort to force words out of my dry mouth while my body began to sweat was a lot to deal with in that moment. After a few minutes, which seemed like an eternity, the ordeal was over. A round of applause from everyone for my effort. Whew! On my first test, which was a spelling test, I received a C+, which is slightly above average by US school standards, but I was disappointed. I should have made an A, but my classmates thought it was pretty good. The school placed me, the other Yugos, and other foreigners in an ESL (English as a Second Language) class. This class would help us with basic grammar, vocabulary, and conversational English. The school helpfully added an additional class specifically for the Yugos that was taught by one of the Bosnians that had been in the States for several years and knew the language. On top of all this, my father would drag me to an English night class with him twice a week at one of the local universities. All of these classes helped, in addition to the day-to-day stuff at school. But in the following summer, the true linguistical transformation happened. During summer vacation, children are typically out of school for about two and a half months. I spent the entire summer watching cartoons with my little sister while my parents worked. Cartoons helped me become a fluent English speaker in a way that formal language classes never could. My brain absorbed the simplicity of the dialogue and words when I was able to focus on English that felt like fun instead of work. Upon returning to school to start the 7th Grade, my classmates were shocked that I sounded completely different and that I could speak English fluently. As you probably can imagine, kids are quicker to pick up new languages than adults, which meant that many times I would translate and interpret for my parents, whether it was sitting at the kitchen table to pore over documents received in the mail or going with them to some government office to talk to a secretary or clerk through a glass screen while barely being able to see over the counter. Even mundane things like asking for directions were my responsibility. I was the interpreter and relished the role. I was the link between the Bosnian language and the English language as a kid and a teenager. This carried on into adulthood but to a smaller and less frequent extent. But translating and interpreting was the most important function to me in my younger years. My family depended on me in these situations, and I stepped up to the plate and performed my duty.

I encountered another school culture shock in 7th grade – paddling. Paddling is another word for corporal punishment. The teacher would take a paddle and impose physical discipline on students who committed a grave infraction. In other words, the teacher would assault the student. One day, the class was unruly and the teacher ordered everyone to write a repetitive sentence expressing their regret hundreds of times and to have it turned in the next day to her. I refused on principle to do this. I wasn't unruly so I wasn't going to write lines. Well numerous kids refused or didn't complete it so the teacher called us up individually to a separate room where another teacher was present to watch and hit the student on the buttocks a few times with a paddle. When it was my turn, I went, got hit a few times and that was that. It didn't really hurt but the concept was humiliating and befuddling.

Sometime after our arrival in the States, we tried to convince my maternal grandmother and my paternal grandparents to join us. They did not want to venture to a new continent, I suppose due to their age, or perhaps fear of the unknown. Our communications with them would continue on a weekly basis where every Saturday we would call them to chat and to see how they were doing.

Unfortunately, my maternal grandmother suffered from health problems. She died in November 2000. I remember waking up that morning. It was a Thursday. There was a cold front hitting the area. I remember my mother waking me up to go to school, in tears, informing me that my grandmother passed away. Of course, you could imagine the shock. This was the first time I experienced death in the family. Here I was 12 years old, in tears, that my grandmother had passed away and I did not get a chance to say a proper goodbye. On the way to the bus stop, I was still in tears. Getting on the bus, I sat next to my Kurdish friend, Jesse. We developed a friendship based on our mutual hobby of professional wrestling and we had been friends for a couple of months at that point. His family came over a couple of years before due to them being Kurds from Iraq. With Saddam Hussein in power in Iraq and his lack of affinity for Kurds, Jesse and his family left. In addition to wrestling, we had similar immigrant experiences in common. He was my first real friend in the States. After noticing my demeanor and my tears, he asked me what happened. I told him. He expressed his condolences and provided me with words of comfort, which helped with the crying. Although it felt like I had a hole in stomach, I felt slightly better.

Now something else happened in 7th grade --- my first American "soccer" experience in physical education class. After a quick warm up and stretch as a group, we were left to organize ourselves. By popular demand the class usually ended up playing either American football or basketball. American football did not interest me, and the sport was not necessarily favorable to boys of my small stature, but every now and then I would venture forth from the relative safety of the sidelines. Since we were not required to participate, there were always some students just sitting beside the field to watch and chat with friends. It was in front of this small audience that I scored a game-winning touchdown. I found myself unmarked on the blindside and raced towards the endzone unnoticed by all except our quarterback, whose pass found me just about on the five-yard line. Perhaps the other team discounted me due to my general disinterest in their beloved sport, but by subverting these expectations, the game winning touchdown spurred my teammates on and they jumped on me to celebrate. As they surrounded me to jubilantly slap my back and rub my head, I had mixed emotions that I can only describe as joy but also frustration that we weren't playing real football! Basketball was a bit better, and at least it has some following in Europe, particularly in the former Yugoslavia. Still, it was nowhere near the level of soccer. As an immigrant, I was itching for the beautiful game to be played at school. I had not played since being in Germany. I could not wait to show the Americans this part of my identity and that I just did not excel academically. As luck would have it, a new teacher came along and wanted the kids to try out a variety of different sports. My Cuban buddy and I were licking our lips. It was time to shine. The other kids had no background in the sport, so we ran roughshod over them. I felt alive for the first time since I arrived in the States. The freedom to perform on the crappy school pitch with *gambetas*, jukes, and nutmegs, scoring goals for fun was exhilarating. I also quickly learned that Americans are not too keen on individual celebrations, or worse, choreographed celebrations by the opposition. They did not see it as me enjoying scoring the goal, but rather me mocking them, which was not the case.

Unfortunately, the teacher's experiment only lasted a week or two, so it was back to square one. But for that one hour for several days, I was in heaven.

My time actually watching the sport was severely diminished. To my knowledge, football was not widely available on TV in the States so following any domestic leagues was out of the question. I do not recall seeing any matches on TV or any highlight shows. The availability of international tournaments (the Euros specifically) was a little bit better though it required paying for it. During the Euros in 2000, we watched a couple of matches at my father's friend's house, whose son ordered some matches on pay-per-view. After regulation had ended, the match went into overtime and eventually penalty kicks. The cable provider ended the coverage and began playing whatever else was supposed to play afterward. The son had to call customer service to get the match back on. American businesses and the American culture were not in tune with the rest of the world with how the sport worked.

With the lack of access to watching the sport, no culture around me to support it, and no one really playing it recreationally, my interest in it dwindled tremendously. I picked up watching professional wrestling as a substitute. I used to watch it on tape delay in Germany regularly and became a fan. Professional wrestling was highly popular at the time. The story telling, characters, and drama were intriguing to me, and my friends and I loved to practice our favorite moves on each other. I also began watching and playing basketball on a regular basis. My passion for football was on the backburner. How long would it be there?

CHAPTER 5

Closure

Čaršija

After not seeing my grandparents for nearly ten years, we now had a green card and enough money saved up to return to Bosnia to visit them for three weeks. One of my mother's cousins picked us up at the airport in Zagreb, Croatia. Banja Luka did not have an international airport so we had to drive roughly three hours before we got to my grandparents' house in Banja Luka. They lived in a neighborhood called Potok. Driving into Potok, one could still see the effects of the war. There was a general air of neglect, and infrequent garbage collection which left large rubbish piles, basically creating a round-about on some streets. Was the government still not functioning properly? Did the government or people do this to invoke *inat* and against whom? For those unfamiliar with the word, it doesn't have an exact definition in the English language. But I will try my best to describe it. *Inat* means hard-headedness, stubbornness, defiance, doing something out of spite, even if sometimes you are hurting yourself in the process or outcome. It can even mean hurting yourself more than your foe. *Inat* can be productive or destructive, depending on the circumstances. It usually involves a bit of drama and theatrics to add to the act. For example, a foreigner in a new country with the deck stacked against him or her invokes the power of the *inat* to show their boss or teacher that not only are they as good as the natives, but better. As curious as I was about the stupid garbage in the street and could never figure out an answer as to why it wasn't collected, my excitement and anticipation of seeing my grandparents again returned to my senses. We drove up a little hill and my grandfather was looking through the window on the second floor watching us drive up. We parked the car and at the top of the stairs, my grandmother and grandfather awaited us. Hugs and kisses were exchanged and of course the waterworks were flowing everywhere. Their house looked exactly like I remembered as a toddler. This was a big deal for my little sister – she only heard of the "grandparents" before but never met them, so the concept finally became real to her.

Later on, my mother's stepfather visited. I remembered childhood trips riding around in his shiny Mercedes-Benz and it brought a wave of emotion to see that car rolling up in front of my grandparents' house. As mentioned previously, my maternal grandmother had passed away less than two years prior, and it was in the Mercedes that we all went to visit her gravesite. On a brighter note, I also met my younger cousin, Vedran. I have always been proud to know that my little cousin was named after me, and when we hugged for the first time, he felt like a long-lost brother. Like a brother, he had an uncanny ability to push all of my buttons. By day two, I was ready to toss him from the window. By day five, his mischievous streak had grown on me. Little Vedran bonded with me so quickly, but as a boy of four or five years, he didn't understand that I wasn't going to be there forever. As we loaded our luggage back into the car three weeks later, he realized that we were leaving and broke down sobbing. I missed him terribly when we had to leave. Most of the trip consisted of seeing family members that I knew and ones I did not know previously and had only heard about. My parents saw old friends. We explored the city, doing some tourist things but mostly going to the places of sentimental value. I especially enjoyed visiting my folks' old hang-out, a part of town called Mala Čaršija (literally translated "Small Bazaar"). These streets were the real life setting of my parents' stories about first dates and young love and happy nights out on the town with friends. I appreciated the fact that I could see where my parents lived instead of just being told about it, or seeing pictures or home video footage of the places where I was from. I could breathe it and live it myself. In the daytime, one gets sucked into a state of serenity when overlooking the Vrbas River from a bridge. Unfortunately, the people don't always live up to the idyllic setting. While sitting in a café, my good mood was shattered by a short, middle-aged man with a combover and a cigarette. In typical, brusque Bosnian fashion, he asked several probing questions about my life and summarily dismissed my dearest dream: "Fourteen? You're too old to be a footballer now."

I passed my time by making acquaintances with the local kids. My grandma was my in. She introduced me to Vladan, a boy my age who knew all the goings-on in the neighborhood. He told me all of the most vital information for a teenage boy, like where to go to find a pickup game of basketball or football with the local boys. The football pitch and basketball courts were next to a stadium where a local lower-division club, FK Naprijed, played their football. It was a ten-minute walk from my grandparents' house. The kids I played against were quite skilled. You could tell that they played on a regular basis. Once word got around that I was just visiting and I spoke English fluently, I was strangely and humorously labeled by one of the kids as "Englez" (Englishman) instead of "Amerikanac" (American). Playing with them, I did not embarrass myself. As a matter of fact, they accepted me on the pitch as if I was one of them. I played like I was one of them too, not selfishly trying to showboat or insecurely trying to prove I was better than the stereotype of an American. I am most proud of how I was able to step back from the "ball-hog" mentality of a dominant immigrant kid absolutely steamrolling the competition in middle school PE, to seeing the kids I was playing with as real teammates. I was able to let go of the impulse to score by my own skill, and I started to be a more thoughtful playmaker. One particularly beautiful assist stands out in my memory. I sent an over-the-top pass from around midfield to a teammate in the box, who chested it down, and poked the ball in the net. I did not know it at the time, but I was channeling one of my future idols, Juan Román Riquelme. The other boy appreciated the assist and my new playmaker role acted as a social lubricant. After the match, he, Vladan, and I went walking around town. They wanted to show me some more of the places that teenagers like. Most importantly, they took me to an internet café. Keep in mind, the internet was still a very new phenomenon in those days, especially in a country that was still recovering from war. Few people used a computer with any regularity, and even fewer owned a personal computer. I missed being connected to the rest of the world and I thought the café was so cool that I went back again later with my family. My sister impressed the people there by demonstrating how she could use computers with ease. The concept of a seven-year-old knowing more about computers than some adults was shocking.

Being in Bosnia felt a little weird. Here I was, back where I was born and raised for the first four years of my life. We spoke Bosnian at home and lived it culturally, but stepping outside of the home, the American culture would infuse itself into our lives. Those three weeks were a taste of what life would have been like had the war never happened or had we stayed. My Bosnian was pretty good but lacked a full lexicon or word fund. While speaking with the locals, I always had little reminders that no matter where I was born or how well I carried on the conversation I was still a foreigner. Some shopkeeper would be making small talk and treating me like any of the locals, but then I would misunderstand some slang or even certain "regular" words and they'd go "oh" in a mix of shock and disappointment. At certain times, it felt like I was being looked at like an American in Bosnia (the opposite was true in the States – a Bosnian in America). I would be caught in this twilight zone of labels from external forces and even within myself. The personal struggle would continue for many years in the search for identity. Questions like "Who am I?" "What am I?" and "Where do I belong?" would occupy my mind very regularly for years on end.

After spending about three weeks in Bosnia, it was time to leave. My dad's cousin happened to be in town, so he drove us to the airport in Zagreb. We bid farewell to my paternal grandparents. Like our arrival, our departure involved many hugs, and tears, and tear-soaked shoulders. Deep down, I knew it was the last time I was going to see them alive, but to comfort my family I said how I hoped there would be more visits in the immediate future. Unfortunately, there were no more visits for me. However, I am grateful now that we had the opportunity to visit at all. We parted ways properly and on our own terms and my memories of them are much more concrete than I was able to form when I was a toddler. It is better to have those memories than nothing at all.

During our sojourn to Bosnia, the World Cup was underway. This time it was being jointly hosted by South Korea and Japan. It was the first World Cup to take place on the Asian continent. Due to the lack of football accessibility in the US, my interest in the sport wasn't the same as it had been in Germany where I could at least watch highlights and select matches. It didn't help that the time difference for this World Cup was huge with Japan and South Korea at a whopping fourteen hours ahead of Alabama. However, bits of news and highlights would filter in throughout waking hours such as South Korea's controversial road to the semifinals and Rivaldo's embarrassing theatrics at the corner flag when Brazil played Türkiye.

The time difference was the major hurdle for me. Alas, I only ended up watching the final between Brazil and Germany. Brazil was still led by Ronaldo "O Fenômeno" who suffered two major career-threatening injuries between the World Cup in France in 1998 and this World Cup. Initially, he ruptured a tendon in his knee in November 1999, against Lecce while playing for Inter Milan. In April 2000, he made his long-awaited return, only for the unthinkable to happen. His knee-cap tendons completely ruptured after being on the pitch for less than ten minutes. Science told the man who was so explosive and was knocking on the door of perhaps being the greatest of all time that his career may be over. He missed the entirety of the 2000/2001 season and only made sixteen appearances in the 2001/2002 season. After surgeries and rehabilitation, Ronaldo defied science and came back, ready for the World Cup, ready to show the world what he was capable of and to exorcise the demons from France '98. This was going to be his personal redemption. He was going to be aided in the attack by his two compatriots, Rivaldo and Ronaldinho.

The Germans were led by Bayern goalkeeper Oliver Kahn, who the German press dubbed "the Titan." Kahn personified anger and intensity on the pitch. He conceded only one goal in the entire tournament up to the final. Germany also had a 24-year-old Miroslav Klose, who scored sixteen goals in the previous Bundesliga campaign for Kaiserslautern and had scored five goals in the tournament. However, one of Germany's key players, midfielder Michael Ballack, would not play the final due to suspension because of accruing a second yellow in the semi-final against co-hosts South Korea. Germany would miss his presence in the center of the pitch.

Waking up at the crack of dawn, I watched the final take place in Yokohama. The match was a back-and-forth affair with both teams having plenty of opportunities. Who would take advantage first? It turned out to be the Brazilians. Rivaldo sent a low-shot Kahn's way, shooting from outside of the box. Kahn was unable to catch it and it rebounded off of him. Ronaldo pounced and was able to get to the ball quicker than Kahn, sending it into the German goal. Twelve minutes later, Brazilian player Kléberson passed the ball to Rivaldo at the top of the box, but Rivaldo dummied it, allowing the ball to go between his legs and find Ronaldo, who sent a very low shot past the sliding Gerald Asamoah and past the "Titan" Oliver Kahn. The match was the story book ending that I wanted for one of my childhood idols. Redemption from the previous World Cup. Renaissance from his injury-plagued years. Ronaldo was a

World Cup winner once again[2], and Golden Boot winner with eight goals at the tournament. Cosmic justice for Ronaldo. Although the Germans lost the final, Oliver Kahn was given the Golden Ball award, which was for best player of the tournament. The Golden Ball award had never been awarded to a goalkeeper before this tournament nor since. Unfortunately, the excitement only lasted a few hours. Football was on the back burner for me once again. Other hobbies such as film, basketball, and professional wrestling were at the forefront of my interests plus the aforementioned lack of accessibility to club football made it hard to get excited for football on a regular basis.

In 2002, it felt like a void had been filled, like there was a completion to a part of my life that had been sitting empty. Returning to Bosnia, seeing my grandparents and others, experiencing life there for a few weeks, filled parts of my soul that needed it. Football-wise, it was glorious to have a proper ending to the Ronaldo saga, to see my childhood idol redeem himself from France 1998, overcoming career threatening injuries, and lifting the World Cup. Brazil's victory was a taste for what once was and what would be again for me in football, although I did not know it at the time.

---

[2] When Ronaldo was seventeen, he was on the Brazilian squad that won the World Cup in 1994, but never saw any playing time.

The next phase of my life would begin one month after the World Cup final; I would start high school. I did not know what to expect. My only expectations again came from American cinema, which I knew couldn't be entirely accurate, but it was my only framework for imagining what was to come. I knew wearing uniforms was going to continue and that I would have friends that were going to attend the school as well but only time would tell how life was about to change. I was nervous but had no other option but to plunge into the deep end and find out.

CHAPTER 6

Lost in the Wilderness

The Middle

Arriving to high school on the first day, I experienced something of a culture shock. My middle school was composed of an overwhelming majority of black Americans. High school, on the other hand, was much more demographically even. Prior to this, most of my interactions on a daily basis were either with my family, other foreigners, or black classmates. Seeing a swath of white Americans was an abrupt departure from what I had considered "normal." Due to the change in my environment and being a little bit older now, I noticed things that I did not notice before. One of my observations was that blacks mostly hung around with other blacks, that whites hung out with other whites, and not only was there an ethnicity component to it, but also an economic class component. The poorer students would usually hang out with each other, the middle-class students would hang out together, and so forth. Sometimes a poorer white student would be part of a group of poorer blacks or vice versa. The same thing happened in other classes, but mostly, the people stuck with their own ethnic group.

As for myself, I was mates with Jesse and his brother, who as previously mentioned were Kurds from Iraq, two other brothers who were from Vietnam and came to the States a few years before me, and a few black and white Americans. As you can imagine, this group was quite diverse. There was still a certain "outsider" feeling on my part. I had been in the States for about three to four years at that point but did not feel like I belonged to mainstream American society. Being friends with other groups of people who were outsiders for whatever reasons of their own created a common bond amongst one another. Our band of misfit boys would play basketball regularly in PE class and outside of school hours.

Although middle school introduced me to the American way of schooling, high school made me notice and question a few things now that I was a few years older. For example, in middle school and high school, school would start somewhere between 6:30 and 7:30 and would be dismissed around 14:30. If you got there early enough, whether by school bus or your own transportation, breakfast would be provided. Lunch was provided as well. However, depending on your parents' income level, one either enjoyed a free meal, a very cheap meal, or a meal at full price which was less than $2. The cafeteria ladies would slop the food onto your tray while the students would line up in a queue. The image my mind conjured up was like a scene out of a prison, where the inmates would be served their meals. The set-up of the cafeteria also contributed to this image in my head with long tables and benches. Also, classes would be the same every day for the semester. The sequence was to have a few classes, then lunch, then more classes. There was no recess. The classes themselves were geared towards memorization and not necessarily critical thinking. Of course, there were exceptions but that tended to be the general course of direction at school. In contrast, the schooling in Germany was different in my experience. The schedule was flexible from day to day, recesses existed, and there was a decent amount of opportunity for students to be creative and free from constant mental restraints. In other words, American schooling bored me. It was mechanical, robotic, mundane, and too routine. I needed a creative outlet.

That creative outlet became film, which was one of those exceptions in high school that I thoroughly enjoyed. I am not sure what triggered my interest in film as an art, but it remains with me still. Part one of the film class was learning about film history, different film theories, aspects of cinematography, and of course watching influential films like *Citizen Kane* and

Casablanca. The second part involved putting the creativity to test with project assignments such as making commercials, animations, and short films. According to my teacher, putting music to film seemed to be my biggest strength with my projects. I became enthralled with film, obsessively watching classic and critically acclaimed films.

Around the same time that the second part of film class was available to take as a subject at school, there were tryouts for the junior varsity soccer team. I figured I should try out and see if I was good enough to make the team. It was a little surreal playing with other boys whose desire was to make the team and who were actually interested in playing the sport unlike my middle school classmates. I was rusty and not fit. I should have planned better for this. After several days of tryouts, I didn't think I was going to make the squad. About a week after tryouts were completed, the coach posted the roster near the gym. As the rumor mill made quick work of this development, hopeful boys quickly excused themselves from their classes to run see the list for themselves. I joined the migration with slower steps, not at all confident that I had made the cut. I stood on tiptoes and peered over shoulders and between heads of the other kids who had tried out, scanning the paper for my name. There it was! My mood flipped in an instant. I was shocked and overjoyed that I made it considering my lackluster performance. I shared a high-five with the boy next to me and took off back to class with considerably more pep in my step. I took a small detour to peep in the window of Jesse's class. He looked up and saw me mouth "I made it!" with a huge grin. His answering grin and thumbs up made gratitude well up within me for having such a good friend to share my achievement with.

What did not occur to me was the amount of time I would have to dedicate to film class and soccer in the same semester. Once I realized this, I was at a crossroads; I would have to choose between my life-long passion or my newest hobby. In one of those decisions that may have changed my life trajectory, I chose film. If I had chosen soccer, I don't know where life would have taken me. Maybe I would be somewhere else. Maybe I would be *someone* else. Perhaps not, maybe it all would have been the same in the end. It is a question that drifts up occasionally on those nights when sleep is elusive and I ponder the consequences of my decision going the other way.

To complicate things, I also had been working a part time job on the weekend. For some, this is a necessity, for others it is a rite of passage, and some simply want something to keep themselves busy and get a little pocket change. Altogether, many middle- and lower-class American teenagers work their way through school and especially summer. In the American ethos, I suppose it is an official start to the principle of "self-sufficiency" and "independence." Personally, I was doing it for pocket money and to help my family out. I was guided towards a pizza chain that the Catholic Social Services rep knew to have hired several ex-Yugos in the past. I started out at the low-end of the totem pole with the unglamorous job of cleaning tables.

As an aside, I want to mention just how many of these confusing phrases like "low man on the totem pole" exist in the English language, and how difficult these idioms are for people trying to learn the language. The majority of native speakers don't even understand this phrase. Allow me to explain. The term "totem pole" refers to a sort of memorial structure traditionally built by some cultures native to the Pacific northwest. Artists carve stylized people and animals (such as a chief or a seahawk) into giant tree trunks, with one image directly above the next, and the part of the trunk closest to eye level is reserved for the most detailed and important figure. So, using this phrase "low on the totem pole" to mean "unimportant" is factually incorrect, but that's the way the language has evolved. For clear communication, you just have to say, "I could care less" and use the words that are familiar to your audience.

Over time, I moved up from cleaning tables to dish washer and a helper in the kitchen. After several years, I was promoted to dough prep and cook. As in middle school, there were a couple of people from the former Yugoslavia working there as well, who had been there longer than me, plus a few Mexicans. My *first* stint there lasted two and a half years.

My parents also found better paying jobs over time, especially my father, who back in the day was accustomed to an office job in Yugoslavia, instead of manual labor at a door production company. He ended up with a job more suitable to his degree. Both my parents worked their asses off to get us where we were. Ultimately, all the hard work paid off and we were able to get a piece of the "American dream" by buying a house.

We weren't the only ones who had achieved some success after several years of being here in the United States. There were other families from Bosnia here of different faiths. We had Muslims, Catholics, and Eastern Orthodox families. The biggest wave arrived between 1998 and 2000, but there was a very small size of others who had arrived prior to this. The overwhelming majority were involved in manual labor as one would expect for incoming immigrants. Of course, they had kids in various age ranges from toddlers to children in their late teens/early 20s. As with us, their living situations improved, better jobs were found and some even formed their own businesses. They would visit each other's houses frequently and help each other out in times of need, whether it was transportation to work or watching each other's children. They would gather at the local Greekfest yearly and you would meet people you didn't know. Like many immigrant communities in the United States, we held on to football as a pastime and as a part of our identity. Eventually, a Bosnian Sunday league team was formed and supporting this team was another event that would gather us together from all across the city. Initially it consisted of all Bosnians with maybe one or two non-Bosnians on the team. This would bring a decent part of the community to attend the matches. I would look forward to attending these Sunday matches as it brought the community together and I could watch football in person. There was a certain amount of pride for me personally at the matches or the annual meet-ups of the community. It felt more natural to me to be in an environment where I could be ethnic and more myself and I didn't have to worry about misunderstandings due to cultural differences with other nationalities or ethnicities. Of course, all good things come to an end eventually. On-field incidents against other teams' players and infighting between teammates caused problems. Certain players did not want to partake anymore. The team fractured. It still existed and other players from different countries joined but it didn't have the same feeling of a Bosnian team anymore as it had previously. Consistent football disappeared out of my life yet again as quickly as it had appeared.

The international tournaments would have to satisfy my thirst for the beautiful game.

In 2004, the Euros came along once again. And once again, it was on pay-per-view. We only ordered the final as each match was around $40 to purchase. The final pitted the hosts, Portugal, against the heavy underdogs and surprise of the tournament, Greece. Now Portugal and Greece both came out of Group A, meaning they faced each other before the final. Their group stage match was the opener of the tournament where Greece shocked the footballing world by beating the hosts 2-1, with goals from Robert De Niro look-alike Giorgos Karagounis in the 7th minute and a penalty scored by Angelos Basinas in the 53rd minute. A goal in the 93rd minute by a nineteen-year-old Cristiano Ronaldo was only a consolidation goal and the Greeks stunned their hosts. Greece was managed by Otto Rehhagel, who took over the team in 2001. Rehhagel had worked miracles before with FC Kaiserslautern in 1997 and 1998, winning the Bundesliga 2 in Germany and immediately after gaining promotion, winning the first division in that season. Rehhagel's philosophy was to adapt his tactics and strategy to play to the strengths of his players. After beating Portugal in the opener, Greece drew with the other country that was part of the Iberian Peninsula, Spain. Greece would fall to the Russians in the last group-stage game and barely advanced as runner-up, due to the tiebreaker of goals-scored as they had more than Spain (both teams had the same number of points and the same goal difference). Greece would face France, the winners of Euro 2000, in the quarterfinals. France still had a sizeable amount of their players from the 1998 World Cup including Zidane, Henry, and Robert Pires. However, despite the star power and talent on the French side, the Greeks were able to extinguish the stars with a defensive display that would ultimately result in a 1-0 victory for them. Another shock vibrated through the football world. Here was Greece, a country that had only qualified once for the Euros and once for the World Cup in their entire footballing history, beating the World Cup winners from 1998 and previous Euro winners from 2000. Greece would face the Czech Republic next in the semifinal. This was the Czech Republic's golden generation with players including Karel Poborský, Tomáš Rosický, Pavel Nedvěd, Jan Koller, and Milan Baroš. The stingy Greece defense pushed the match into extra-time. The silver goal rule, which UEFA had introduced around 2002-2003 was in effect, which meant that if someone scored in the first half of extra time and the other team did not score before the first half of extra-time ended, the match would be over. The Greeks managed to score their winner in the added minute at the end of the first half of extra time from a corner that was headed in by Traianos Dellas. The Greeks were dreaming – they were in the final of the Euros. No one expected them to make it out of the group stage, much less get to the final. Their odds were 150/1 before the tournament. Could they complete the improbable and become Euro champions for the first time in their history? They would have to beat Portugal again to make that happen.

Portugal, on the other hand, was coached by Gene Hackman look-alike Luiz Felipe Scolari, who two years prior to the Euros had won the World Cup with Brazil. Portugal's team was star-studded with talisman Figo, Deco, Pauleta, Rui Costa, Ricardo Carvalho, Maniche, and the aforementioned Cristiano Ronaldo. Portugal had reached the semifinals twice in Euro competition, in 1984 and in 2000. Was this going to be their moment, winning the competition on home soil? Their opening match defeat to Greece was not expected. However subsequent victories over Russia and Spain had them top their group and a date with England in the quarter finals. The match against England took both teams to the distance. After a defensive blunder by Costinha in the 3rd minute, Michael Owen latched on to the ball with an exquisite finish. Portugal was in search of an equalizer for the rest of the match. They would find it in a Hélder Postiga header after a cross into the box in the 83rd minute. The match went into extra time, where the sides traded a goal apiece in the second half, which led to penalties. David

Beckham would miss the first England penalty, but Rui Costa would miss Portugal's third, leading to sudden death. England and Aston Villa striker Darius Vassell would miss, sending Portugal to another semi-final appearance where they would play Holland. Portugal would score first in their match against the Dutch. After conceding a corner, Deco would deliver the ball into the middle of the box for Cristiano Ronaldo to simply head it home past the Dutch goalkeeper Edwin van der Sar. Later in the first half, talisman Figo would almost score a curler, but his effort hit the post and the Dutch could breathe a sigh of relief. However, in the second half, Maniche would be successful with a curling strike from the corner of the Dutch box, making it 2-0 for the hosts. An own goal in the 63rd by Andrade kept the game close with the Dutch missing a golden opportunity to tie the game, but it wasn't to be. Portugal would be in its first final at a major international tournament.

    I did not have a dog in the fight but leaned towards the Portuguese. Their football was more pleasing to the eye than Greece's bunker football. Not much happened in the first half, with maybe a chance here or there. In the second half, Greece would get a corner. The Greeks relished set-pieces in the tournament as it was their best opportunity to score. And they did not miss their chance. An Angelos Basinas delivery would find the head of Angelos Charisteas who rose in the air and headed into the Portuguese net. This forced Portugal to throw attacking wave after attacking wave at the Greek goal, but the Greeks remained resolute in defense. The German referee blew the final whistle. Against all odds, the Greeks were European champions for the first and, so far, only time in their history. Otto Rehhagel pulled off another miracle as he had done previously in Germany with Kaiserslautern in the late 1990s. The Greeks adopted "King Otto" as his nickname and he became an honorary citizen of Athens. The unlikeliest of victors had reared their head and crowned themselves European champions.

 High school was becoming easier over time. In the latter half of my four-year high school stint, I increased my workload at the pizza restaurant, not only working weekends, but also a day or two during the middle of the week. It helped that I was of driving age and could drive myself without burdening my parents. Being of driving age and having a car was a big deal. Public transportation was minimal to non-existent in Mobile. There was a bus line that ran but it was nothing like the ones I experienced in Europe. There were no subways and there were no trolleys. Instead of building up like in Europe, cities in the American South were building outwards. On top of the fact that the distances were farther and it made public transport not as feasible, purchasing a car in the States was cheaper compared to their counterparts in Europe and gas prices were cheaper too. Lastly, it goes back to the American ethos of independence. Having a car brought a sense of freedom not experienced before. I didn't have to rely on my parents or older friends to take me somewhere. The last year or so in high school was routine and more routine. It was school, work, basketball, and film. At this point, I was waiting to graduate and take the next step in life, which would be college for me. For a while and because of my interest in film, I was leaning towards film school. However, with no film school in relative proximity and any move being a huge financial and familial sacrifice, I opted to study business as I could attend one of the local colleges and continue to live with my parents.

As 2006 began, my paternal grandfather was battling health complications. It didn't look good for him. At 3 AM one morning late in January, the phone just kept on ringing and ringing. I already knew what it was about, but I did not want to hear it said. I walked to the kitchen and picked up the phone and my dad's cousin was on the other line. Because my voice had changed since he last heard it several years ago, he thought it was my dad speaking. He was speaking as I was running to my parents' bedroom to wake up my father and told him to hold on. I woke him up and hurriedly handed him the phone and retreated to my bedroom. I wasn't ready to hear the news but overheard my father's part of the conversation. After he finished, he opened the door to my bedroom and confirmed the terrible news. I knew it was coming, but I wasn't ready to accept it yet. After all, is anyone really ever ready to hear of a loved ones' passing? Another grandparent gone, but at least memories other from childhood remained and we had a real goodbye in 2002. That was the part that made the mourning a little bit easier. This left my grandmother alone without a husband, my dad without a father, my mother without a father-in-law, and myself and my sister with no grandfather. After the period of mourning and burying him, we had to figure out the next question – what were we going to do to with my grandmother's living situation?

The spring of 2006 approached, which, as always, felt like the great outdoors had leapt directly from winter to the height of summer. Late spring typically means crawfish boils and graduation parties in backyards and along riverbanks across the South. My high school graduation ceremony was finally here, though I didn't participate in the traditional American celebration. We weren't integrated into that part of the culture yet, so our post-graduation plan was different that some others' and we simply ate at a restaurant afterwards. Due to the mass of people that attend these graduation ceremonies, it was held at one of the local colleges, which I would begin to attend in the fall of 2006. Of course, the ceremony included the famous "Pomp & Circumstance", a processional piece present in practically all high school and college ceremonies in the States and an orchestral version of "Move Along" by the All-American Rejects. I couldn't help but think of Randy "Macho Man" Savage's entrance to the wrestling ring during the playing of the former piece and imagining myself imitating him when my name was called to walk across the stage, snickering to myself while the thought crossed my mind. A few speeches were given by the administrators and the valedictorian, and we began to queue up for our name to be called so we could walk across the stage, shake hands with the principal, and grab our diploma (which was just an empty booklet meant to hold the degree that would get mailed to us later) in our all-white graduation gowns and caps. Luckily for people with foreign names, they made sure that we went up to the announcement team prior to the ceremony to tell them how to pronounce our name. It was a very friendly gesture to avoid people's names being butchered in front of their families. The ceremony was followed by obligatory pictures with friends and family members and congratulations from the same. To me, finishing high school was just the next step in my academic career – it was only half-time for me. Expectations were that I would go to college and, personally, I had the innate drive that I needed to go forward and aim higher than high school. My high school grades were well-above average, but this was without me trying my best. I could've put more effort into my schoolwork than I did, but school wasn't particularly exciting, and my hobbies and passions took precedent. Maybe university would be different.

Before college would start in August, another World Cup was about to take place. This time around it was hosted by the country that had previously hosted *me*, Germany. This was a reinvigorated and younger German team coached by Jürgen Klinsmann. The French had an older Zinedine Zidane and boasted others like Thierry Henry, an aging Claude Makélélé, Patrick Vieira, and Lilian Thuram. Brazil still had a somewhat declining Ronaldo with protégé Ronaldinho being the star of the team now. Their South American neighbors, Argentina, also had plenty of talent on show with the great number "10" Juan Román Riquelme as the leader and playmaker of the team and a very young Lionel Messi making his World Cup debut. Last but not least, Italy. They had depth in every position and their play was orchestrated by Andrea Pirlo. I don't recall such a star-studded World Cup like this with legends. It proved to be epic.

I spent my summer working full time at the pizza restaurant while trying to catch matches when I could. Without being emotionally involved in the football, I sort of followed Italy's

World Cup run. With the time difference and working quite a bit, there would be times I could catch a match before going to work or even at work itself on the TV set there. Making a dough ball of pizza and peaking my head out from the door that led to the "back of the house" of the restaurant to catch a glimpse of the action going on the TV was a very common tactic of mine at work during the tournament. Naturally when I worked in the front area of the restaurant, I would be able to catch more action. Controversial penalty for Italy in the 95th minute against Australia with Totti scoring? Watched near the hot oven in the kitchen with pizza sauce and cheese on my shirt and apron.

It was unusual for me to watch the latter stages of the tournament without my dad. The World Cup had always been a father-son event for me. He had the familial obligation of rearranging my grandmother's living situation in Bosnia due to my grandfather's death earlier in the year. With no other soccer fans around, it was a rather lonely time. His absence bothered me. The event had not been complete without him, but there was nothing else I could do except try to enjoy it by myself.

The tournament had been rolling along with all the traditionally big football nations making the knockout stages. There were not any real surprises in the group stages except for maybe World Cup debutant Ghana making it out of the group stage with Italy in Group E and Croatia bowing out in Group F. In the round of 16, Germany dispatched Sweden 2-0 with Zlatan Ibrahimović on the losing side. Mexico would take Argentina to extra time when a Maxi Rodriguez wondergoal sealed the match for Argentinians. The Italians met Tim Cahill's Australia. The Italians played for nearly all the second half with ten men after Marco Materazzi was given a straight red. With seconds to go in regular time, Fabio Grosso would find himself in possession near the right side of the Australian box. He dribbled past one defender; a second defender slid in but did not take Grosso out. Instead, Grosso fell over him. The Spanish referee pointed to the spot and Francesco Totti stepped up. The camera zoomed in on his piercing blue eyes for a moment as if this was the final shootout in a spaghetti western. Australian goalkeeper Mark Schwarzer guessed correctly and dove to the correct side but he was helpless to stop the precision and power behind the ball. Italy was through. A tasty match up of Spain against France produced a total of four goals. Spanish striker David Villa put his country ahead via a beautifully placed penalty to Barthez's right after a foul was committed by Lillian Thuram on Pablo in the box. Thirteen minutes after taking the lead, Patrick Vieira found Franck Ribéry making a run and produced a throughball. Ribéry rounded Iker Casillas and struck the ball into the net. The deadlock was broken in the 83rd minute after Zidane sent in a free kick into the Spanish box. The ball hit the head of a Spanish player where it then found Patrick Vieira at the far post who headed the ball towards the net. The ball actually hit Sergio Ramos on the way in, but Vieira was credited with the goal. While time was ticking away, Spain threw their players forward. The French were able to launch a quick counter with acres of space in the Spanish defensive third. Zidane entered the box with his graceful touches, dribbling past Carles Puyol and sending a powerful, low shot past his Real Madrid teammate Iker Casillas. The French were through to the quarter finals. History was made in the round of 16 match-up between Brazil and Ghana. Although the match finished 3-0 for the Brazilians, it wasn't the scoreline that made headlines. Rather, it was for Ronaldo breaking the World Cup goalscoring record. In the 5th minute of play, a Ghanaian offside trap was broken by Ronaldo's perfectly timed run and Kaká's throughball. The legendary 9 in trademark fashion latched onto the ball and rounded the keeper with a scissor move and kicked the ball into the open net. This was Ronaldo's 15th goal at the World Cup finals, breaking the previous record of Germany's Gerd Müller in Müller's home country. Brazil's victory meant that they would face Zidane's France in the quarterfinals.

In the quarterfinals, the hosts and my former country of residence would meet Argentina. I remembered Argentina from the 1998 World Cup with their beautiful sky-blue and white jerseys and my dad talking about them and the legend of Maradona occasionally. I had respect for this nation. They were to be taken seriously with their history and football heritage. Argentina maintained the majority of possession, picking and probing to see how they could find the killer pass to get an opportunity to score. Juan Román Riquelme, Argentina's great ten and string-pulling playmaker, dominated the midfield and Argentina's action would run through him. Riquelme used his frame to protect the ball and retain possession. You could tell his football intelligence was above the other players on the pitch. He would see three to four moves ahead or see things that no one else would see on the field. A little flick here and there, an open teammate out of nowhere, a simple touch of the ball to progress it further up the field – these things made him a spectacle to watch. He was truly a maestro on the ball. Finally, Argentina would find a way though, but through a set piece. A corner taken by Riquelme found the head of center-back Roberto Ayala in the 49th minute. With Argentina leading 1-0 and about 18 minutes left to play in the match, a momentary lapse of reason would turn out to be very costly. With perhaps the worst substitution in the competition's history, Jose Pékerman, the manager, took off Riquelme while Argentina had the lead. Instead of putting another attacking player on who could retain the ball and put pressure on the Germans such as Pablo Aimar or Lionel Messi, he went defensive and inserted Esteban Cambiasso into the mix. While Cambiasso is a great player, the nature of the game needed something else. With no one to control the midfield for Argentina, the Germans equalized in the 80th minute through Miroslav Klose. This led to extra time and ultimately penalties where the Germans were perfect from the spot and Argentina missed through Ayala and Cambiasso. This denied the footballing world a matchup between Italy vs Argentina, a matchup between two great playmakers in Andrea Pirlo and Juan Román Riquelme. The football fan in me always ponders the "what if?" had Pékerman not taken out Riquelme. For the Italians, their quarterfinal was not so dramatic. It was a breeze as they dispatched the Ukrainians 3-0, with a brace from Luca Toni. They would face the Germans in their semifinal match-up at the Westfalenstadion in Dortmund.

In the other half of the bracket, France would play the reigning champions, Brazil. In the late spring, Zidane announced that he was hanging up his football boots after the World Cup, so football lovers wondered what kind of performance they would get from "Zizou." And Zidane did not disappoint. He put on a masterclass against the Brazilians. This was a man determined to make his swansong go down in history. He ran France's midfield with the assistance of Patrick Vieira and Claude Makélélé against Brazil's Ronaldinho, Kaká, Juninho, and Gilberto Silva. His deft touch, feints, and dribbles while always managing to retain the ball wowed the crowd and the TV audience alike. While both teams were threatening in the first half, there weren't any true clear-cut chances and the goalkeepers weren't called into action much. But the breakthrough came in the 57th minute. From a set piece, Zidane found Thierry Henry completely unmarked at the back post. Henry smashed the ball into the roof of the net and France was up with a little over half an hour to go. France had a couple of more chances to seal the victory, including one where the ball rolled across the face of the Brazilian goal, but no one was there to tap it in. Later in the match, a Ronaldinho free-kick was close to going into the net but went inches over the bar. Dida was forced into another low shot save and Ronaldo tested Barthez on the other end, but the French keeper parried the ball away. France held on and earned themselves a spot in the semifinal.

The Germans would face Italy in the semifinal on the 4th of July. This was one of the few days that the pizza joint was closed for business because it was Independence Day in America. With no school and no work, I would enjoy this match without interruptions in my small bedroom in our home. It turned out to be an epic match. This was a great historical rivalry with the weight of wins in the Italians' favor. The last time these two nations met at a World Cup prior to this match was in the World Cup Final in 1982. That match was highlighted by goals from the great Paolo Rossi, Marco Tardelli (and his iconic celebration of absolute joy after scoring, which ended up being one of the most memorable World Cup moments of all time), and Alessandro Altobelli, who dispatched the Germans in a 3-1 victory to claim their third World Cup. The Germans had the home advantage so things would be slightly in their favor. The Italians had most of the possession and eleven shots on goal compared to Germany's six. Jens Lehmann was forced into ten saves during the match, from distance and from up close. The first half involved a lot of back-and-forth action, with both teams threatening each other's goals, but most of these shots were off target. The story was the same for the second half. So, the match went into extra time. The Italians threatened immediately after the restart with Alberto Gilardino who was subbed in for Luca Toni, getting past one defender on his way to the box, and dribbling past another in the box, before sending a shot that beat Lehmann but hit the post. The Italians were getting closer. Only a minute or so later, Gianluca Zambrotta hit a powerful shot from the edge of the box that smacked the crossbar. At the end of the first half of extra-time, Lukas Podolski had a free header to put the Germans up, but his attempt went wide. In the second half of extra-time, Buffon was forced into a big save from Podolski as the forward found himself with space in the left side of the box and hit a powerful shot towards the goal. Buffon just managed to get a hand on it, sending it over the crossbar. On the other end, a few minutes before the whistle, Pirlo forced a save from Lehmann from distance.

With the game tied in extra time and appearing to head to penalties, Italy had a corner that was taken by Alessandro Del Piero. He delivered into the danger area, but it was headed away, landing at Pirlo's feet at the top of 18-yard box. A moment of genius from the midfield maestro found Fabio Grosso in the box with plenty of space around him. He curled the ball past Lehmann in the 119th minute and into the net. Grosso channeled his inner Marco Tardelli in his celebration. The same joy and emotion on his face as if Tardelli himself was on the field. The Germans were stunned. Just two minutes later, with the Germans throwing everything up front, Italy hit them on the counter. Gilardino held up the ball and passed it with a deft touch to Juventus legend Del Piero, who drilled the ball into the top right corner past the hapless Lehmann. The Germans and their fans were in tears. It was game over. Italy was going to the final.

In the other semi-final that took place the next day, France faced Portugal with an aging Figo and a young Cristiano. Both teams played attacking football in the first half, but the defining moment of the first half and the entire match came around the 33rd minute when Thierry Henry was brought down in the box by Ricardo Carvalho. Zidane stepped up and with a very short run-up, if you could even call it that, found the back of the net. Portuguese goalkeeper Ricardo guessed the correct way, but Zizou's shot was too powerful and precise. In the second half, Henry had a chance out of the gate, but Ricardo did enough to send the ball out of bounds. Not too long after, Ribéry tested Ricardo from distance with the goalkeeper saving it. The Portuguese threatened the French consistently. A trademark Cristiano free-kick went straight at Barthez who could not hold on to it but the follow up header by Figo went over the bar. In injury time, center-back Fernando Meira had the ball headed down to him in the opposition's box, but he skied it way over the French goal. The Portuguese had a few corners afterwards but couldn't produce any danger out of them. In the dying seconds, Portugal was denied a chance while they were through on goal with a correctly adjudged off-side call. France and Zidane were going to their second World Cup final in eight years, and they would face the Italians in Berlin.

The French have had the Italians' number for years. Italy had not beaten the French since the World Cup in 1978 and their previous meeting in the Euro 2000 final was a victory for Les Blues. It was a warm Sunday evening in Berlin's Olympiastadion as the teams made their way onto the pitch. Less than 7 minutes into the match, Materazzi made minimal contact with Florent Malouda in the box, but it was enough for the Argentinian referee to point to the spot. Zidane (who else?) stepped up and shot with a Panenka-style penalty which hit the underside of the crossbar but crossed the line after it hit the grass. Advantage to the French. I was rooting for the Italians and even though this was very early in the match, it made me nervous. Every time Zidane would have the ball, I would be terrified. However, my nerves were soon spared – the lead lasted only about 12 minutes. Andrea Pirlo sent a corner kick into the box, and Marco Materazzi redeemed himself by rising above the opposition's defense and meeting it with his head to guide the ball past Fabian Barthez. The Italians almost recreated the goal when Luca Toni hit the crossbar after another Pirlo corner. In the second half, Henry bedazzled the Italian defense and crossed it over to Florent Malouda, but Zambrotta arrived and booted the ball out of bounds. Later on, Malouda was brought down in the box by Zambrotta, but the ref did not deem it a penalty. The Italians on the other end gained a free-kick; Grosso's delivery would meet Luca Toni's head, who put it past Barthez, but he was deemed to be offside. Again, the French would respond with a threat of their own as Henry fired a low shot towards Buffon but the goalkeeper parried it away. The match finished 1-1 in regulation and we were headed to extra time.

Two chances for the French materialized. A shot by Franck Ribéry went wide after a nice intricate give and go with Florent Malouda and a Willy Sagnol cross found an open Zidane in the box who headed it on target, but Buffon made another great save to deny France's number ten. However, the match gained notoriety for what happened with Materazzi and Zidane in the second half of extra time. While in the penalty box during a French attack, words were exchanged where Zidane offered Materazzi his jersey after the Italian was holding on to briefly. Materazzi responded that he preferred Zidane's sister. This enraged the latter so much that he head-butted the former in the chest. The assistant referee saw this and alerted the main referee, who promptly pulled out the red card from his back pocket. Zidane in his last ever match, a World Cup final in extra time, received a red card after being unable to keep his emotions under control. It shocked the football world. After being given his marching orders, Zidane walked down the tunnel past the World Cup trophy – it created an unforgettable image. Does losing his cool in perhaps the most important match of his career affect Zidane's legacy? You tell me.

With not much happening afterwards, the match went to penalties. Pirlo would step up first and convert his, and so would Wiltord for the French. Materazzi converted his as well. On the French side, David Trezeguet, the French-born striker of Argentinian ancestry, stepped up and fired a powerful shot but it hit the underside of the crossbar. Unlike Zidane's penalty at the beginning of the match, the crossbar was not a friend to France this time and it clearly bounced outside of the goal-line. Both teams would exchange scoring penalties after this. Italy's fifth and decisive penalty would be taken by Fabio Grosso, scorer in the semifinal. And Grosso stepped up to the challenge, converting his shot. The Italians were world champions for the fourth time in their history. Both teams were worthy finalists and the match lived up to the hype.

It was a year for endings and beginnings. It turned out to be the last World Cup for many stars who had dazzled and etched their names into the annals of football history like Ronaldo, Zinedine Zidane, and Juan Román Riquelme. But new ones came along who made their first World Cup appearance, including Lionel Messi, Cristiano Ronaldo, Luka Modrić, and Wayne Rooney. When my dad returned, he brought me back a Juventus jersey with the name "Ibrahimović" on the back. I had no idea who this guy was at the time, but it was my first kit since I had been in the States and unbeknownst to me, the start of my collection and the first seed planted in my mind to remember the name Ibrahimović. Ultimately, it turned out to be a summer of working a lot and missing my dad while he was away doing his familial duty. I stepped up and did my own familial duty by helping my mother around the house and working. My time in high school was over and I would start college that fall. What I could not predict or expect in my next life chapter was that a certain professor would forever change me.

CHAPTER 7

Out of the Darkness, Into the Light

Blackbird

The all-too-familiar heat and humidity in August was unmerciful on the first day of college. That day was unusual for me. For someone who thinks of himself as a planner and having some foresight into actions and consequences, that day was a mess. I failed to consider the traffic that morning. Once I arrived, I had no idea where to park my car. Once I figured that out, I wasn't sure what building to go to since two of them were next to each other and shared the same name. And lastly, I was late for my first class. The joke that morning was on me. I had to plan better for the next day.

Starting college brought a couple of more visual changes. As opposed to uniforms like in middle school and high school, people wore whatever they wanted. The appearance of the campus itself too involved a lot more green space and nicer, more aesthetically pleasing architecture. It did not have a feeling of constriction and tightness, at least appearance wise. The college naturally had a lot more students than what I was accustomed to and, a little surprising to me at the time, the racial make-up tilted heavily towards whites. I figured it was going to be somewhat like high school in terms of demographics, but that wasn't the case.

I started my college career with the intention of getting a degree in business administration. I really had no idea what I wanted to do after I finished high school, but getting an American college degree was of utmost importance as my parents expected me to obtain one. Since I had no idea what I wanted to do, I figured I might as well get the similar type of degree as my father had done back in Bosnia.

The basic college courses I took for my degree didn't excite me. There was no inner desire or urgency that made me look forward to them. Those were just routine along with the pizza restaurant gig. Life was just going on autopilot for the school year. It seemed like there was nothing more to life at this point. Life just seemed kind of empty, without meaning, and I was aimless. While the aimlessness made its presence known in my mind and soul, another milestone passed and for me, the highlight of the year. We had lived in the US for long enough that we could apply for American citizenship and so we did. In the spring of 2007, we received notice to come to Atlanta to take the citizenship test. A pamphlet was provided to cover potential test questions that dealt with American history, civics, and government. Upon making the 5-hour trek to Atlanta, we arrived at some nondescript government building. There were dozens of others there with the same mission. We all went individually into separate rooms with a proctor. The test consisted of less than 5 questions about the topics provided to us in the pamphlet and writing a few sentences to demonstrate that you could write in English. The whole thing was over in less than ten minutes. The test seemed a lot easier than any of us anticipated...we didn't even have to wrestle a mountain troll. After we were informed that we passed, we had to wait for what seemed like an eternity in a big, ceremonial room to take the oath. When the moment came, it was quite solemn. The oath was administered, and we repeated every word. We were now officially Americans. It felt strange. One culture, my native one, was pulling me in one direction and the American culture in the other. It was like Dr. Jekyll and Mr. Hyde and I had to find my identity within it.

While I was roaming through life at the time like a lost puppy, one of the required courses was an introduction to government class. Entering my second year of college, the professor walked in the first day of class, slightly hunched over and shuffling his feet, an older man in his 60s. His face was somewhat tan with reading glasses. There were liver spots on his hand. He was a native New Yorker and Jewish and carried a heavily northern accent. His teaching style was in-your-face direct, very frank, and he would raise his voice. The lectures included open-ended questions, where you hoped your answer was right, otherwise your head and soul would swell with embarrassment in front of the whole class. The whole thing was intimidating. His name was Dr. Ethan Fishman and for about half of the semester I hated him.

I did not look forward to his class. In fact, I dreaded it. I didn't want to be embarrassed in front of the other students. This went on for about half of the semester until I realized I was looking at it from the wrong perspective. First of all, I was learning things, despite his style, and he was different than any other teacher or professor I ever had. Two, I needed to stop caring as to what my fellow students thought. After all, why should I care about some stranger's opinion? Lastly, I realized that the key was not to take things personally. That made the difference, and I was off to the races. I finally came around to realize that this man was a very good professor. I approached him one day after class to see what else he taught. He said he was teaching a couple of classes next semester that I wasn't eligible to take yet because I hadn't taken the first part of those. But he told me that in the summer, he would teach the first part of his political philosophy class.

Unfortunately, after the fall semester was over, my maternal grandmother succumbed to her health complications. Issues related to her diabetes had plagued her for many years, and she died in December 2007. All the grandparents were now deceased, and we did not have any close relatives that tied us back to the former Yugoslavia. It was almost like a break with the past, a break with certain parts of cultural and personal identity. There was nothing left for us in Bosnia but ghosts and memories. This certainly added to the aimlessness that I was experiencing.

The spring of 2008 came and went like the crane flies. It was time to sign up for summer classes and I did not forget to sign up Dr. Fishman's "Political Philosophy I" class. I was looking forward to the summer to see what the class had to offer. It was khaki shorts and a t-shirt type of weather as usual. I was nervous. Would he remember me? Would I be able to meet the challenge of another Fishman class? Or would I fail and walk out of there with my tail between my legs? The number of students in the class was small as expected for the summer so it made the lectures more personal and more intimate. The subjects for the semester were Plato, Aristotle, St. Augustine, and St. Thomas Aquinas and their greatest writing "hit" in political philosophy. He would explain the underlying assumption and view of reality that these great thinkers based their philosophies on, respectively. He would teach via the Socratic method. This meant that he would ask specific questions about the material or even generic questions about it, where one would or should arrive at the answer naturally as the answer was based on the teaching of natural law, the classical realist view of reality, and human behavior. While answering or thinking about the question, one would also gain some knowledge of one's inner self and discover a truth. He was teaching us to think completely differently and outside of the box. He knew the answers were within us and he was just bringing them back out of us into the world. Then he would tie it together with the course material or even contemporary political events or modern, societal behavior. This wasn't your run of the mill classroom. This man, who cared about his students, wanted us to think critically about ourselves and the world we lived in, and he wanted us to feel alive. Where I realized all of this was at some point in the earlier part of the semester when he was lecturing. I can't recall what point he was trying to make, but he said that his class was kind of like "Life 101" and it felt like something had awoken me out of some deep sleep that I had been in for years and years. I shook my head as one would shake their head when someone startles them. I got it. I truly got it. Everything made sense at that point. It was exciting and I felt alive. I even discussed all of this with my parents, whereas before I had never really discussed school material with them. They were pleasantly surprised to see such enthusiasm from me. Dr. Fishman set me on a path to success. My grades went from good to excellent in all subjects. He gave me this mystical energy where I wanted to perform to the best of my abilities. I took more courses with him. They became like a mental booster that kept me going. We also became good friends. I would visit him in his office down the hall from the classroom to discuss class material with him or even just chat with him. He became like a surrogate grandfather to me.

Due to Dr. Fishman's influence, I changed my major from business administration to political science, which allowed me to take additional courses with him. I was still working at the pizza joint as well and had a consistent schedule. I sort of gained seniority at work, having worked there for roughly 4 years or so, and did not have to work on Saturdays. This allowed me to do any homework for the following week. When I was done, I would catch my father watching football. Football was becoming more readily available on television in the United States. Italy's Serie A was his choice, specifically Intern Milan, and he would point out Zlatan Ibrahimović to me. Zlatan piqued my interest with his 6'5" frame, exquisite footwork for a man of his size, and of course his Balkan name. This would become a ritual and time for father-son bonding; each Saturday or Sunday, we would watch Inter because of Zlatan Ibrahimović.

Ibra brought me back to watching football on a regular basis. I finally had something to hold onto in football again.

Detour - About Zlatan - The Lion King

Zlatan was born in Malmö, Sweden to a Bosnian father and a Croatian mother. His parents divorced when Zlatan was a child, growing up in the Swedish ghetto. Due to being an outsider, he fought to survive – he became a warrior. He would assert his dominance on the streets and the fields with his football skills and big personality, something that he would carry into his professional career. Because he was an immigrant of a lower class, he would clash with Swedish kids, who he felt looked down on him. This anger and desire to prove himself fueled Zlatan and it became his motivation. You could say he was fueled by the power of *inat*. The *inat* is sometimes displayed in his interviews through his brash and confrontation style. For some distinguishing Zlatan the character and Zlatan the man is difficult as his humor is dry and style of answering questions comes off across as arrogant. He would call it confidence. The fact that he was of Balkan descent, was an underdog growing up, and carried a chip on his shoulder struck a chord with me as I saw myself in that situation many times, whether it was in Germany or the United States. I had to prove to my classmates and coworkers that this immigrant would try his best to show them that I was every bit their equal, if not better.

Zlatan would start his professional career at Malmö, then move to Ajax, from Ajax to Juve, from Juve to Inter, from Inter to Barcelona, from Barcelona to AC Milan, from AC Milan to PSG, from PSG to Manchester United, from United to LA Galaxy, and finish his career off at AC Milan. Over a nearly 25-year career, he would win an incredible number of accolades, both on an individual and on a club level. I would follow Zlatan for the rest of his career, not necessarily supporting any team that he played for, but hoping he would do well and dazzle us with his football magic. And impress fans he did. He was a human highlight reel, scoring fascinating goals on a regular occasion, but my favorite performance was Sweden's friendly against England on November 14, 2012, while Zlatan was plying his club trade for PSG. Zlatan scored all four goals for Sweden. The fourth goal will live on in football history. A ball was heading to the English defense. Zlatan ran after it, but goalkeeper Joe Hart rushed out and headed it away. Zlatan anticipating what Hart was going to do, backed off, and let him head the ball. Then Zlatan using his taekwondo skills and acrobatics jumped in the air, hitting a bicycle kick from what appeared to be nearly 25 meters/ 27 yards out. The ball went in. I had never seen such a goal before or after this in my life. I was flabbergasted. This goal would win the Puskas Award for the goal of the season. In addition, this was Zlatan's middle finger to the English media that doubted him. And to remove any inkling of doubt by the same media, Zlatan moved to Manchester when he was almost 35 years old. Over nearly two full seasons, in which the second one was hampered by injuries, Zlatan would make 53 appearances, scoring 29 times and assisting 10 times, across all competitions, helping United win the League Cup, the Community Shield, and the Europa League. This was an example of Zlatan's mentality that he had to prove his doubters wrong like he did when he was a teenager on the streets of Rosengard in Malmö. Age would catch up with Zlatan during his second stint with AC Milan, when in his fourth season, at the age of 41, injuries would consistently plague him. On June 4, 2023, a tearful Zlatan announced his retirement from football in front of a full San Siro crowd after their last game of the season. It was a bittersweet moment. It was time for Zlatan to say goodbye, but it was difficult to see this legend call it quits on his playing career.

Back on Track

In my second to last year in college, with Dr. Fishman's influence, I decided I needed something more than just a bachelor's degree. My ambitions became greater. I decided on graduate school. That meant I needed to continuously keep my grades as high as they were and start to research and apply to various schools. Soon graduation was on the horizon, a semester earlier than it should have been due to me driving like a Ferrari through college, at breakneck speed. The ceremony was scheduled for December 2009. I was looking forward to having my family see me up there on stage and see the conclusion of my undergraduate career. They would be proud of me obtaining my college degree in America, as the first *real* part of my formal American education. I also looked forward to Dr. Fishman attending the ceremony – the professor who brought out the best in me, to see his work (me) walk across the stage to receive my diploma. Unfortunately, when the day came, my wishes of having all the influential people watch me didn't come to fruition. Dr. Fishman was absent. It turned out he was sick. However, my reunion with Dr. Fishman would happen several months later under surprising circumstances.

In the meantime, it was time to say *ciao* to the pizzeria. After nearly half a decade cleaning tables and dishes, making dough and other items on the menu from scratch, stretching the dough, making the pizza, and cutting it, and working the cash register, it was time to move on. The pizza sauce stains on my shirt would be no more. That smell that the restaurant produced and that would stick to my clothes and the inside of my car would finally be gone. At one point, the higher ups tried to convince me to take on a managerial position, but I politely declined. I had other ambitions. I made the switch over to work with my dad while I applied to different graduate schools.

I took an exam administered by a national organization as a requirement to get into graduate school. The results weren't good. I winged it with minimal studying. I got what I deserved for the time that I put in. I went ahead and applied to graduate schools and planned on retaking the test in a couple of months. Time was ticking to get into schools, and I certainly did not want to waste a year and a half not moving forward career-wise. It was stressful and I did not want to fail. After studying much more consistently over the next couple of months, the day finally came. Springsteen's *The Rising* would be the soundtrack over to the test site as I hoped it would inspire me and energize me to do well on the test. The results were sent to the schools that I applied to. After waiting weeks, the results were better than the first time around, but still not to my liking. On top of that, the first couple of rejections came in. I felt down and out, hopeless. I was consumed by getting into graduate school. I kept asking myself if I was going to be accepted anywhere. There was only one school left to hear from. I needed a day off from work for some tranquility and relaxation in order to try not to think about the situation. So I decided to go to a little island that was a short distance from the city. I brought a little lunch and a chair to lay on while reading a magazine. It was difficult not to think about the future even though I tried my best not to. Staring out into the empty sea towards the Southern hemisphere brought me a feeling of serenity and calm. The direction I was staring at was perhaps foreshadowing for later in life. There was something on the horizon that lent me a measure of comfort against the stress that was crushing my heart. I don't know what it was but it proved calming and therapeutic. After spending a couple of hours at the beach, I returned home and turned on the desktop to check if there was any update from the last remaining school. I logged on to the portal and there *was* an update…I had been accepted! The moment of screaming relief hit me like a dump truck. I called my parents to let them know of the news. They were ecstatic for me. My biggest worry at the time had been wiped away.

While waiting to go to graduate school, in the spring of 2010, I was notified that I was being inducted into the national political science honors society. This would take place on my former college campus. I thought it was a nice honor and I would see Dr. Fishman again and catch up with him. Upon arrival, I was handed out the program for the ceremony. It turned out, and Dr. Fishman kept this a secret from me, that I was going to get the student of the year award in the political science department. I could not believe it. I was flabbergasted. Apparently, all the professors had to take a vote to determine this outcome and Dr. Fishman campaigned for me. I felt like this was me getting the equivalent of the World Cup or Ballon D'Or or the Academy Award for Best Actor. If I were Juan Román Riquelme, Fishman would be my Carlos Bianchi; if I were Robert De Niro, Fishman would be my Martin Scorsese. His tutelage brought out the best in me. Pure joy just flowed through me. All my hard work and eagerness to learn paid off as I was finally able to get recognition. I was on the mountain top and I didn't want to come down. It was my moment of glory.

After a small reception, I returned to work and let my father know what had just happened. He gave me a tight, congratulatory hug. I told him I also got a little check of a hundred dollars as part of the recognition. He said to me "Jebeš pare, ovo drugo je bolje" ("Screw the money, this other thing [recognition] is better"). And I felt the exact same way.

The boss at work knew that I was accepted to graduate school and would be leaving a few months down the road. The company was also trying to cut costs due to new technology being available, making my job unnecessary. A few weeks before the World Cup was about to kick-off in South Africa, the company laid me off with a continuity of pay for a certain amount of time plus a severance package once said pay ended. It turned out that I would get paid while I could enjoy my summer with the World Cup and other things before I departed for graduate school. What more could I ask for at the time?

The 2010 World Cup was the first to be held on the African continent. Colombian pop star Shakira provided the theme song called "Waka Waka ("This Time for Africa"). The crowds created a bee-hive sound through an instrument called the vuvuzela during EVERY match for the WHOLE match. It wasn't pleasurable to the ears, at least mine anyway. The typical favorites included Germany, Spain, Argentina, and the Netherlands. Spain's squad had been dubbed their "golden generation" and they were the incoming European champions, known for their tiki-taka style of play. Argentina were coming to the World Cup with arguably the greatest player of all time, Diego Armando Maradona, as coach and Lionel Messi as his protégé and star of a stacked team. The Netherlands also brought star-power with Arjen Robben, Robin Van Persie, and the Inter Milan treble winner, Wesley Sneijder, as their most important players.

I recall quite a few memorable moments from the group stage. Spain came into the tournament, losing one match out of 26 since winning the Euros in 2008. That loss, a surprising one, came against the United States at the Confederations Cup in 2009. Spain would start their World Cup campaign against

Switzerland but suffered a shock defeat against them courtesy of a Gelson Fernandes goal. This served as a wakeup call for the Spaniards. They would win their other two group stage games against Honduras and Chile respectively and qualify as group winners. Uruguay, who had not been a football power in decades on the international stage, had their own golden generation with Luis Suárez and Diego Forlán. Uruguay's overall solid squad topped their group with France. France, finalists in 2006, qualified for the tournament by going through the playoffs by beating the Republic of Ireland in controversial fashion after Henry handled the ball in the Irish box and then passing it to William Gallas who headed it into the goal. There was infighting in the French camp between the coach Raymond Domenech and certain players. On top of all that, certain players didn't make the call-up like Karim Benzema. The French team imploded, losing to Mexico and the hosts, South Africa, and drawing with Urugay. They were out. The hosts themselves did not qualify out of the group but their opening goal against Mexico in the tournament's opener scored by Siphiwe Tshabalala was iconic with the post-goal celebratory dance, the crowd going absolutely bonkers, and Peter Drury's memorable line "Goal, Bafana Bafana! Goal for South Africa! Goal for all Africa!"

Argentina would win all their group games and finish at the top. However, they too had difficulty qualifying for the World Cup, finishing 4th in CONMEBOL qualifying and narrowly avoiding having to go through the intercontinental playoff. Argentina was managed by Diego Maradona who took over the team from Alfio "Coco" Basile (then in his second stint as gaffer). Basile had previously coached Argentina from 1991-1994, winning the Copa America in 1991 and 1993, the Confederations Cup in 1992, and the Artemio Franchi Cup in 1993. Legendary players, even if they are in the pantheon of the GOAT conversation, do not necessarily make great coaches. Case in point, some of Maradona's decisions were questionable as he failed to select Javier Zanetti and Esteban Cambiasso, treble winners with Inter Milan that season into the squad. Moreover, a public feud ensued between him and Juan Román Riquelme, where the latter ultimately decided their differences were too big and did not want to play for Maradona's Argentina.

My country of residence, the USA, was in a group with England, Slovenia, and Algeria. In the US's opener against its mother country, the match ended a 1-1 draw. The match is remembered for an absolute howler committed by English goalkeeper Robert Green in the 40th minute when Clint Dempsey shot on goal from outside the box. Green was ready to just catch the ball from the ground as it was a low shot. Unable to catch it, the ball bounced off his hands and into the net. The US performed quite well against English opposition, who on paper appeared to be better than their American cousins, but on the pitch, the Americans proved to be formidable opponents. In their third group stage match, the US needed a win against Algeria to qualify for the knockout stage. A draw would not do. Algeria hit the crossbar early on after a defensive blunder. Dempsey scored but the goal was nullified after he was adjudged to be in an off-side position. He would hit the post later as well. The Americans were pushing for a win. The game reached the 90-minute mark and there were 4 minutes added on. In the 91st minute, after Tim Howard saved a header, he threw the ball out far to Landon Donovan who was sprinting down the pitch. He found Jozy Altidore on the right who centered it for Dempsey, but the Algerian goalkeeper and Dempsey met the ball nearly at the same time. The ball bounced back out to an oncoming Landon Donovan who slotted it home to qualify for the knockout stage. With Ian Darke's commentary of "Go, Go, USA!" the American players celebrated in a huge pile near the corner flag. It was an iconic moment in American soccer history.

Germany finished at the top of their group although they suffered an unexpected defeat to Serbia in their second game while their neighbors, the Netherlands went undefeated in theirs. Traditional powerhouse Italy continued the shocks in the group stage as they finished at the bottom of their group that included Paraguay, Slovakia, and New Zealand. Brazil and their Lusophone cousins, the Portuguese, were drawn in a group together but finished first and second respectively.

Old foes Germany and England faced off in the round of 16. The Germans scored through Miroslav Klose and Lukas Podolski. Matthew Upson got the English on the scoreboard via header by a Steven Gerrard assist. Controversy showed its face in the 38th minute. Frank Lampard shot from outside of the box. The ball hit the underside of the crossbar and clearly crossed the goal line. The ball bounced into the goal and back out. The whole world saw it. Replays showed it was a clear goal, but the ref didn't give it nor did the linesman indicate that it crossed the line. Lampard's goal would have made the match 2-2. In the middle of the second half, Germany scored two goals through Thomas Müller within minutes of each other and that was all she wrote. Lampard's goal that wasn't given perhaps restarted the conversation for goal line technology that would begin to be implemented in late 2012.

Another pair of foes faced off in the round of 16. It was the Iberian derby between Portugal and Spain. "La Roja" came out swinging. David Villa and Fernando Torres tested the Portuguese goalkeeper several times in the first ten minutes.

Portugal too had chances later on in the first half, testing Iker Casillas from afar. An entertaining first half finished goalless. The first real chance would come for Spain in the 60th minute – Sergio Ramos played a long ball to giant Fernando Llorente who dived in to head the ball, but goalkeeper Eduardo kept it out. Only a couple of minutes later, Spain got their breakthrough after some intricate passing around the Portuguese box. David Villa, who was most likely in an offside position after receiving a backheel pass from Xavi, shot at goal. Eduardo saved it, but the rebound came back to Villa who shot it into the net. Spain were up 1-0 and the score would remain the same for the rest of the match though Spain had a couple of more chances to increase the scoreline. Spain marched on to the quarters. Cristiano and Portugal were out.

If the World Cup needed a villain in human form, then it would have to be Uruguay's Luis Suárez. After a hotly contested round of sixteen match against the United States, Ghana, the only African team who made the knockout stages, would face Uruguay. I wanted Ghana to advance. I wanted them to carry the banner for the entire African continent. I wanted the underdog to move on. Uruguay threatened early on in the match and it took Ghana until about thirty minutes in to threaten Fernando Muslera's goal. But in stoppage time in the first half, it was treble winner with Inter Milan, Sulley Muntari, who would strike from way on out. It was a low curling shot that bounced past Muslera. The Black Stars were on the scoreboard! However, the lead wouldn't last very long. On the other side of half-time, Diego Forlán scored a beautiful free-kick past Kingson to equalize. Suárez had a chance to score for Uruguay, but Kingson saved his shot. The match would go to extra time and here was where it would become one of the most dramatic matches in World Cup finals history. Late in extra time, Ghana had a set-piece. The ball ping-ponged around in the six-yard box. Stephen Appiah got his head on it, and it looked like Ghana would take the lead, but Luis Suárez blocked the ball with his hand, preventing it from crossing the goal-line. I became so enthralled in the match that I was pacing back and forth in the living room. The ref noticed and gave Suárez a straight red and a penalty kick for Ghana, for all of Africa. Ghana now had the chance to put the match to rest via Asamoah Gyan. Luis Suárez slowly made his way towards the tunnel in tears. Gyan stepped up and send a powerful shot down the middle, but it hit the crossbar. I sunk my head into the pillow on the couch out of frustration. The Black Stars played well. This should've been it, but the football gods had other plans. Suárez began celebrating at the tunnel's entrance. All of Ghana hated him and probably most of Africa too. Gyan's miss turned out to be the last kick in extra time and the game went on to penalties. On penalties, Maxi Pereira would miss for Uruguay after Mensah had missed for Ghana. It was up to Adiyiah to even the score, but he too, had his penalty saved. Abreu stepped up for Uruguay and sent a Panenka towards the goal. It was as if time slowed down drastically. Kingson could do nothing as he dived out of the way. The ball hit the net and Uruguay were through. The Ghanaian dream was over. The African dream was over. There were no more teams left from the African continent in the World Cup. Luis Suárez introduced himself to a global audience as a villain. The match had drama, it had goals, it had a story that developed as the match went on, and it had controversy. All of this mixed together made it an iconic match not to be forgotten.

Argentina was demolished by the Germans in the quarter final. The Germans scored off a set-piece three minutes into a match when Bastian Schweinsteiger sent the ball in and Thomas Müller headed the ball past "Chiquito" Romero. It took Argentina a while to settle into the match. The Germans continued the onslaught, even after they had scored the initial goal. Argentina managed to send the ball into the net before half-time, but the goal was offside. Out of the gate in the second half, Di María sent a bullet past Neuer but the ball went wide. The flood gates opened in the 68th minute. Klose tapped the ball into the net and Friedrich followed up in the 74th. Klose would get his brace in the 89th minute. The Germans handily beat the Argentinians. Messi and co. were out. It was very disappointing. The dream of having Maradona, arguably the greatest player of all time, lift the World Cup again as coach next to his protégé Lionel Messi turned into a nightmare. Maradona's selection mistakes and tactical acumen were exposed. I am not sure, had Riquelme, Zanetti, and Cambiasso been called up, whether that would've ultimately made a difference since Maradona's tactics weren't up to par. Playing Monday morning quarterback here, had Maradona accepted a role as Basile's assistant (had it been offered to him in the first place) and those aforementioned players had been called up, Argentina would've had a legitimate shot at getting to the final and perhaps winning it all. A final between Argentina's midfield against Spain's midfield would've been mouthwatering. But alas, it wasn't meant to be.

Germany would face the Spaniards in the semi-final. Spain had beaten Paraguay after another goal from David Villa in the quarterfinals where the ball rebounded to him after Pedro hit the post. Villa himself then hit the inside of the right post, the ball bouncing off that post to the left post and then bouncing into the net. In the semis against the Germans, Tarzan look-alike Carles Puyol came crashing in off his vine in a set-piece situation and headed the ball past Manuel Neuer into the net in the 73rd minute. Spain was in their first ever World Cup final.

Spain would face the Netherlands. The Netherlands won all of their group stage matches. They beat Slovakia in the Round of 16 before beating Brazil in the quarters 2-1. They faced off against Uruguay in the semis, where they beat the South American outfit 3-2. The Netherlands had been to the World Cup final in the past, losing to Germany in 1974 and to Argentina in 1978. This meant that the winner of this World Cup final would be someone who had never won it before. I was hoping that Spain would pull it off. I really enjoyed their style and liked their players, particularly Andrés Iniesta, David Villa, and Xavi Hernández.

There was one big footballing connection between these two countries and that was the legendary Johan Cruyff. He made his name in the Netherlands through footballing giant Ajax, winning the league six times in his first stint and winning the European Cup, the predecessor to the Champions League, three consecutive times. He was a runner-up with the Netherlands at the 1974 World Cup where they lost to Germany. He transferred to Catalan giants FC Barcelona in 1973 and helped them win La Liga that season which they had not done since 1960. After hanging up his boots, he would manage Ajax as well as Barcelona. He coached Barcelona to four consecutive league titles starting in 1990-1991 and led them to victory against Sampdoria in the 1991-1992 European Cup final, Barcelona's first. This was dubbed Cruyff's Dream Team with Ronald Koeman, a certain Pep Guardiola, Hristo Stoichkov, and Michael Laudrup all starting in the final. Cruyff's philosophy that he built on from Rinus Michels' philosophy at Ajax, when Cruyff was himself a player, was called "total football." "Total football" meant that each player was not fixed to a certain position on the field. It meant that the style depended on intelligent and technically adept players who could move from place to place on the field as required without jeopardizing the organizational structure of the team. FC Barcelona played a version of this, with heavy emphasis on retaining possession and ball movement, and it worked. It was dubbed tiki-taka. It was aesthetically pleasing to watch and highly effective. And since Barcelona had many players who played for the Spanish national team, Vicente del Bosque, the Spanish manager at the time of the World Cup, built on this philosophy. Spain had been successful at the Euros in 2008 with Luis Aragonés utilizing a version of this style of football and this World Cup was a continuation of that.

This should've been a final where two countries with historically similar football philosophies would produce magic on the field. However, the Dutch didn't get the memo. The Dutch turned into bruisers against the Spaniards, while the Spaniards themselves carried the mantle of beautiful football. It was akin to trying to watch an orchestra perform while they were disturbed and irritated by hecklers. Netherlands' intense pressing and fouling did not allow the Spanish to perform their best version of tiki-taka. It was shocking that it took so long for someone to get sent off, especially after Nigel De Jong kung-fu kicked Xabi Alonso in the chest. The first (and only) sendoff happened to be Johnny Heitinga in the 109th minute after a second yellow. Spain themselves weren't entirely innocent throughout the match, but you could see which side tried to play football and which side didn't. With one man up, the Spanish pushed for a winner. And it was in the 116th minute that the tension that built up throughout the entire match would find a release. The Spanish attack started from their own half. Eventually the ball made its way to Fernando Torres, who attempted to cross the ball to the great Andrés Iniesta. That cross was blocked. However, Cesc Fàbregas got to the rebound first, finding Iniesta open. Iniesta took one touch, let the ball bounce in front of him and struck it beautifully and just in time – an oncoming tackle from Rafael van der Vaart attempting to block the shot was milliseconds too late. The ball flew past goalkeeper Stekelenburg and into the net. As Iniesta was celebrating, he took his shirt off to reveal "Dani Jarque Siempre Con Nosotros [Dani Jarque Always With Us]", a fellow professional footballer and a friend of Iniesta's who died at the age of 26 of a heart attack. In my parents' living room, the release of emotion and high fives between me and my dad was at a crescendo. We wanted Spain to win. Spain was a deserved winner, after years and years of underachieving. They finally won the biggest prize in football with a goal by someone who deserved to score it: El Ilusionista, el Caballero Pálido - the great Andrés Iniesta. The Dutch were criticized by Cruyff himself and others in the papers for their anti-football while the Spaniards were celebrated for winning with class and style. Beautiful football had won and I loved it.

CHAPTER 8

On My Own

Learning to Fly

A month after Spain lifted the World Cup trophy, I would begin again, but this time on my own, when I moved away to start graduate school. A couple of weeks prior, we rented a moving truck and moved personal belongings into the apartment that I found near the school. The parking lot was surrounded by brick walls and barbwire fencing on top of the wall and the entrance to the parking lot had a gate. The front entrance to the building required a badge to get inside and so did the back entrance by the pool. It was a six-story building, and the hallways were just unattractive. They were old and made of white-painted cinder blocks. The apartment itself was small, smaller than anything I ever lived in. The entire setting gave off vibes of a refugee camp. Here we go again. After we schlepped everything up to my new apartment on the fifth floor, we made our way back to Mobile. The whole ordeal took 15 hours.

Orientation for school was going to start in a week or two, with classes beginning just a few days after. I was dreading the day I was going to have to leave my family and my home. I never had to live on my own before. We had been a tight-knit unit all of our lives so me "leaving the nest," and putting a decent-sized distance between us was difficult. It was clear to me how attached I was to my family.

The first few weeks I had a hard time adjusting, but once school really began, classes and studying overtook any emotions of being homesick. I had never had to study like this before or pay attention in class every second of the lecture hour. It was challenging. That first semester was incredibly difficult. At times, I thought this challenge was too much for me. I wanted to give up and throw in the towel. In a moment of last resort, when I felt down and out, I called my dad to let him know about all of this. He told me not to give up, don't surrender. I had to be reminded that we had been through more difficult things in life than graduate school. If we did not give up then, how could I give up now? After a long pep-talk with him, he inspired me to continue and fight against the obstacles in the way. I felt energized and ready to move forward.

Graduate school improved as the year went on, and I became ingrained in the routine. I had acquaintances and a girlfriend. I even joined an indoor soccer league, with a team formed by some classmates who had somewhat of an interest in the game, but were not fanatics like me. I would travel back to visit my family regularly throughout that time. I missed my mother's cooking. That smell of *pita* (thinly rolled phyllo dough that forms a pastry) that would permeate the air on Sunday mornings, whether it was *burek* (beef filling) or *zeljanica* (spinach filling) – would be a staple of my homecomings. It was something I could not replicate. She would send a whole cooler of food with me, which would normally include the *pita*, *ruska salata* (Russian salad), and *sarma* (stuffed cabbage). If I had any dirty laundry that I brought with me, she would do that for me as well. She made sure her baby boy was taken care of before I left to go back to school. It had been like that all of my life, but I didn't really appreciate it as much until I had moved away for graduate school. I missed seeing my family and spending time with them.

Naturally, school couldn't consume my life. I needed an outlet and of course it would be football. Football was more widely available on TV than it had been years prior. It also kept me close with my father despite the distance between us. After loving the way Spain played at the World Cup and following Zlatan Ibrahimović when he moved to Barcelona for a single season, I continued following the Catalonia based outfit. It seemed to be the proper transition with Andrés Iniesta, Xavi

Hernández, David Villa, amongst many others, playing for the national side and for Barcelona. And of course, there was the Argentinian "La Pulga" Lionel Messi. The Barcelona side played the most beautiful football that I had seen up to that time. The tiki-taka brand of football where the emphasis was placed on retaining possession, passing the ball and moving yourself to an open position, then finding the killer pass and the teammate was like listening to a perfect orchestra. Those players and that brand of football kept me tuning in each and every week.

I also turned my attention to South American football. GolTV in the States carried a lot of South American football in the late 2000s. This typically covered the Primera in Argentina, the Brasileirão from Brazil, and the Uruguayan league. Mi padre watched River Plate during the time of Gonzalo Higuaín and Radamel Falcao. Other team names would come up during these matches, including Boca Juniors. Although I didn't watch these matches with him, passing through the living room, I would hear the name "Boca Juniors." It stuck. Why did it stick? I have no idea, but I'll call it fate.

Not only would my interest begin in South American football in graduate school, but destiny also allowed me to meet someone from the continent there. Once the summer came, there were whispers of a Brazilian moving into our apartment building. I confirmed the rumors with the elderly landlord. As I parked my car one day, I saw a big Brazilian flag hanging from his window. My first introduction to him was a happenstance encounter in the building's elevator a week or two later. He definitely did not look "American", and I hadn't seen him before so I could only assume he was the Brazilian in the building since he looked like the Brazilian football players I watched. With us getting on the elevator together to go to our respective floors, my first words to him were "You from Brazil?" He nodded in the affirmative. The next question was "You watch football?" while kicking out my leg to make sure to differentiate between the American version of football and the global one. The chances he would say yes were high since he was from the country where they *joga bonito*. Of course, the next question then was "Pelé or Maradona?" The answer was "Pelé, God, Maradona." A friendship kicked off. Since he had no car, I would regularly take him grocery shopping with me or wherever else he needed to go. My family and I depended on transportation in the States when we first arrived, so this was my way of paying it forward. We shared similar values and a similar outlook on life; he wasn't American and although I was an American on paper, I didn't necessarily feel like one. The culture was still foreign and strange to me in many ways. So having a friend who was closer to me in outlook, values, and culture was a godsend. We were both also homesick, so our friendship had another commonality that we found and connected through. He was a brother from another mother to me. His name is Juliano.

During our time in school together, he would tell me stories of Brazilian teams and other big teams in South America. When time allowed during our busy schedule, we would watch the occasional Flamengo game as that was the club he supported and other big matches in South America. I would be introduced to my first Superclásico. River Plate vs. Boca Juniors. The match took place on October 28, 2012. I don't remember anything about the match itself, but an overhead shot of El Monumental. I thought the aesthetic of it was very bland and its gray color scheme made for a dreary sight. Our love for football did not just involve watching matches together. I also got him to join the indoor soccer league with me and in one match, I assisted one of his goals. We celebrated by copying Bebeto's iconic "rock the baby" celebration from the 1994 World Cup.

We topped off our football adventure together by watching the UEFA Champions League final between Borussia Dortmund and FC Bayern München. I was pumped for this one. I restarted my following of BVB somewhat in the season prior when they annihilated Bayern in the DFB Pokal final. It was a little surreal watching them as an adult again due to the long break in-between when I stopped following them and restarted. They were in a group with Real Madrid, Ajax, and Manchester

City. They topped the group quite unexpectedly, the highlight being when they outplayed the Spanish giants in both games without fear. They beat Ukrainian side Shakhtar Donetsk in the round of 16 before coming up against Spanish side Málaga in the quarterfinals.

Málaga had been purchased by Sheikh Abdullah ben Nasser Al Than in 2010 and he invested heavily in the club. Málaga's players were no slouches. Dortmund's team had won the previous two Bundesliga seasons with their heavy-metal football and gegenpressing tactics, orchestrated by the charismatic Jürgen Klopp. The first match in Málaga finished 0-0. It was the second leg in Dortmund that would prove to be memorable. The match was tied at half-time at 1-1 with goals by Lewandowski for Dortmund and Joaquín for Málaga. In the 82nd minute, Eliseu scored from a clear off-side position, but the goal was allowed to stand. BVB had to score two now to advance. Klopp subbed in centerback Mats Hummels to send long balls into the box. And it worked! In the 91st minute, the ball found itself at Marco Reus's feet in the box and he slotted it home. Was it too late for another one? The football gods allowed a non-call to go in Dortmund's favor. In the 93rd minute, Lewandowski sent a ball into the box. After some ping-pong in the box, Felipe Santana tapped it home. Santana was off-side when he scored the goal. Injustice had occurred to both teams, but equalized itself out. I had the match on after class that day and witnessed this comeback. My emotions came undone after Santana's goal. The tears flowed. Here I was reconnecting emotionally with my childhood team after a very long absence and perhaps the nostalgia that I associated with it. The European nights where I eagerly watched Dortmund as a kid, sitting on the floor of the refugee camp, were back. I could not wait until the semis to see if the campaign of 1997 would repeat itself. But Dortmund had a tough task ahead of them; they were paired against Real Madrid yet again.

Would Dortmund play against their semifinal foes like they did in the group stage? Yes, they would and then some. Dortmund took the lead in the 8th minute after Lewandowski tapped in a cross. Near the end of the first half, Real would pounce on a Mats Hummels error and Cristiano slotted it home to make it 1-1 before half time. After half-time, Dortmund needed to respond and respond they did. Dortmund scored in the 50th and 55th minute from open play and sealed the match in the 66th via penalty. All the goals were scored by Robert Lewandowski. I couldn't believe how easily Dortmund had dispatched the mighty Real Madrid. The heavy-metal football was too much for the Spaniards. After this performance, I chose to believe that the win in 1997 would repeat itself, but they had go to Madrid first and play the second leg, which turned out to be a very tense affair. Ultimately, Dortmund lost 2-0 and Real had chances to complete their comeback but they could not capitalize on them. Dortmund was going to the final, which was to be played at one of football's cathedrals – Wembley Stadium in London. And they would face their domestic rivals Bayern München who brushed Messi's Barcelona aside in the semis with an aggregate score of 7-0.

Juliano and I met with some Brazilian buddies of his that he met in town. It was nice to watch the final with people who had football in their blood and culture. The match itself proved to be one of the most entertaining Champions League finals in years. Dortmund came out of the gate, pressing and starting their heavy metal concerto with gusto. Bayern initially played very measured. The match was quite open throughout with lots back and forth action and both goalkeepers having to make saves in the first half. In the 60th minute, Bayern would score first after Robben found Mandžukić in the box who simply and awkwardly slotted it in. The score would not remain as such for very long. Bayern defender Dante fouled Reus in the Bayern box and Dortmund was awarded a penalty. Dante was already on a yellow and it was befuddling why he didn't receive a second yellow and his marching orders after kicking Reus in the lower abdomen. It may have had changed the trajectory of the match had BVB been up an extra man. İlkay Gündoğan slotted the ball past Neuer who went the wrong way. Bayern had a chance after Thomas Müller centered the ball for Robben, but Neven Subotić cleared it off the line in perhaps the most dramatic goal line clearances I had ever seen. I exploded with joy from my seat. Bayern kept pushing on and they were the better team in the second half. The clock was ticking and the match appeared to head into extra time, but in the 89th minute, a long ball was sent into the Dortmund box. It found Franck Ribéry who back heeled the ball to an oncoming Arjen Robben, who wriggled himself through a couple of Dortmund players and sent a low, weak shot past Weidenfeller. The ball rolled slowly into the goal. And that was it. It was not meant to be a repeat of 1997. Around the world, Dortmund fans' hearts broke in unison, including mine. It was a depressing ride back to the apartment.

As for Juliano, his time in the US was coming to an end and he was returning to Brazil. The parting gift that he gave to me could not have described the Brazilian culture better: a football and a case of beer. I dropped him off at the local airport and we exchanged hugs. My brother had left, but I knew deep down that I would see him again and that our friendship would last. My interest in South American football went with him for the time being. It's much easier to be interested in a league when there are comrades who share the same interest and if the league is easier to access on TV.

CHAPTER 9

Despair

Atlantic City

As the torment that was graduate school was coming to an end, I had to start looking for work in my field while also having the state exam on the horizon. With the work market being too saturated, it was difficult finding something or even hearing anything back. Even getting a letter stating the company wasn't hiring was better than not hearing anything at all. Once the official studies began for the exam, I had to treat studying like a full-time job. This went on for almost two months. Studying in the morning, then a lunch break, then more studying, then a dinner break, and more studying. I may have had 2 hours to myself per day for all of this. On the weekends, I allowed myself a little leeway to unwind before jumping right back into the grind. A couple of days before the exam, I was done with my studies. If I hadn't learned it by now, I wasn't going to learn it this late. The day before, I needed to physically distance myself from my study space in order to relax, so I went to a park quite far away from my apartment. I took the ball Juliano had given me and kicked it around, pretending I was Andrés Iniesta. I felt a strange overlap between the solitude of being in the park by myself, while surrounded by other people, as well as the solitude of studying for and preparing to take this exam, while feeling the love and support from my family in Mobile and now Brazil, too. It was very therapeutic and calming to just play around with a football and to take my mind off what was coming next.

The exam day seemed like a blur. I had no idea how I thought I performed. All I could do was my best. Of course, there was the fear that I had failed and would have to retake it, but worrying wasn't going to help me in the least. I continued applying to several companies while awaiting results. It was the same deal as before. Mostly no responses, some responses indicating they weren't hiring, and an occasional interview with negative results. It was frustrating. I finished my schooling with good grades and various relevant job experiences. It seemed like none of that carried any water. I hoped the results would help and eagerly awaited the day they would be announced. And when the day finally came, I was highly anxious. Clicking the refresh button on my browser incessantly, the link to the list finally appeared. I saw my name on the passing list and felt the relief that washed over me. Now that I passed, I would continue applying for work with full certification on my resume.

However, nothing changed on that front. In addition, with classmates moving on themselves, there was nothing left for me personally or professionally in Mississippi. A month after getting results back, I moved back to Mobile with my family due to financial reasons. Personally, I felt like a failure. Here I had a graduate degree and was certified in the field, but I couldn't find anyone willing to take a risk hiring a new graduate. I had to come up with plan B. I decided I was going to try my job search in Alabama. While doing so life was at a stand-still. All of it felt monotonous and empty. The longer the search continued without any results, my optimism began to dwindle. Just sitting around and waiting for a rejection to a job application was better than not hearing anything at all. The situation was frustrating. It was probably the most meaningless my life has ever felt to me. I just existed and it didn't feel like I was progressing towards anything. The only silver lining I had was my family and football.

Football helped cure the search for employment blues on a temporary basis. Watching the underdog Atlético Madrid with their staunch defense and knife-between-the-teeth mentality go at it every weekend with their competitors was a good distraction. Diego Simeone's team mirrored their coach's mentality when he was a player himself. The players gave it 100 percent each match, physically and mentally, because if you were going to defend for most of the match, you would have to stay mentally sharp. The team was rough and rugged. The front line was headed by Spanish national team record-goalscorer David Villa who had been recently acquired from Barcelona and Brazilian Diego Costa who would make a name for himself in the season with his pace, power, and grit. The midfield was marshaled by Koke with support from Gabi, Tiago, and tricky winger Arda Turan. The heart and soul, however, was the defense with Uruguayan Diego Godín being the leader and Juanfran Torres and the two Brazilians Miranda and Filipe Luís completing the back line. Between the sticks was the Belgian giant, Thibaut Courtois. The bench was also deep with Cristian Rodríguez, Diego, Mario Suárez, and others who seemed ready to die for the cause. It was rather different from the type of football that I enjoyed a couple of years prior. Watching the tiki-taka, orchestral Barcelona side and comparing it to the bunker style of Atlético Madrid was going to extremes. Now I enjoyed the survival mode in football exemplified by Atlético. Maybe because I was doggedly determined to survive myself. On top of that, it was refreshing to see a change of pace in La Liga with someone challenging Barcelona and Real Madrid's hegemony.

Football continued to keep me in good stead after I moved back. My father, two of his buddies, and I took a trip to St. Louis where Argentina would face Bosnia in a pre-World Cup friendly. The country of my birth would face the country that I had a very soft spot for because of their football. Bosnia qualified for their first World Cup since becoming an independent nation, so it was a big deal to face off against the great Argentina, in what was essentially a home match for Bosnia, to test the waters ahead of the World Cup in Brazil. Why would it be a "home match" for Bosnia? A lot of Bosnians settled in St. Louis after the war in the 90s and in 2013 that community had grown to around 70,000 or so. The Bosnians even have a little part of town akin to Chinatown in Los Angeles or Little Italy in New York City. I was looking forward to all of it. We arrived the day before the match after a ten-hour drive. The first order of business was to get some authentic Bosnian food. We ate at a popular spot called Grbić. The place was full and the atmosphere was jovial. I had to get my hands on a dish called *ćevapi*, also known as *ćevapčići*. *Ćevapi* look like small sausages that are traditionally eaten with *lepinja* (a flatbread which is fluffy and soft), raw chopped onion, and *kajmak* (a cheese-based spread). The *ćevapi* are minced meat (the type of meat used varies regionally) usually served in a group of eight to ten pieces. The food just hit the right spot. While this wasn't my first time eating *ćevapi* in a restaurant in the States, it was a rare occasion for me and this was easily the most memorable because of the excitement of our trip and the good company in which I was able to enjoy the food.

The next day before the match festivities began, we walked around the Bosnian area of town and consumed more Bosnian delicacies. There was Bosnian music coming from shops and the streets were full of people wearing the national team's regalia. Trucks would drive by with the Bosnian flag waving. In addition to the Bosnians who lived in St. Louis, there was an influx of Bosnians that came to the city specifically to watch the match. It was an ocean of people. While I was hanging around other Bosnians and hearing my native language, some phenomena – let's call it social osmosis – recalled and improved my forgotten Bosnian vocabulary. It was a strange effect that I wasn't expecting at all. Another strange effect that I have noticed is if I am speaking Bosnian, my personality changes. It is like I become another character. As if I am method-acting, a chameleon, changing far more than just the language I speak to match my surroundings. It is the same when I am speaking English. The tone of my voice changes, my mannerisms change, and I begin to think in the language I am speaking. A transformation takes place.

After spending the afternoon in the Bosnian area of town, it was time to make it to the match. The game itself was held at Busch Stadium where the St. Louis Cardinals play baseball. It was incredibly cold and we wore thick jackets. As I've said, although the country of Bosnia was thousands of miles away from St. Louis, it was definitely a home match for the blue and yellow Dragons. The Bosnian ultras named the BHFanaticos brought the noise to the stadium and created a raucous atmosphere. I was excited to see players from both teams like Ángel Di María and Kun Agüero for Argentina and Miralem Pjanić and Edin Džeko for Bosnia. However, most of the Bosnian players themselves put in an incredibly lackluster performance and phoned it in. But for Sead Kolašinac, no one looked like they were ready to die for the badge on the pitch. Maybe because it was the middle of the European season or maybe because the Argentinians were better or maybe they just didn't care. Tactically, there was no one to protect the back four and Argentina ran rampant in midfield. It was very disappointing and irritating from a Bosnian point of view. Argentina, without Lionel Messi, stole the show with Di María and Agüero. Seeing Di María on the television and in person are two different things. He absolutely mesmerized and terrified the Bosnian defense. When it came time to score, it was Agüero's turn to stamp his authority on the match. Palacio latched onto a ball but goalkeeper Asmir Begović came out to stop him. While taking Palacio out, the ball bounced off the two men and Agüero, ever the opportunist in front of goal, slotted it past Begović and between two Bosnian defenders. Later, in the earlier stages of the second half, Agüero perhaps should've been sent off for lashing out at Emir Spahić after the Argentine thought Spahić's challenge was too rough. He kicked out at Spahić and made contact with the back of his leg, but the referee didn't see it and then refused to see it even after the Bosnian players were pointing to the replay that was being shown on the big screen at the stadium. It was deliberate and worthy of a red card. Less than ten minutes later, Agüero finished the match off with a beautiful bullet of a half-volley, silencing the Bosnian crowd in the stadium. The match finished 2-0 for the Albiceleste and it was a well-deserved victory.

The day after the match, we overheard a story that took place the night before. A Bosnian man had traveled from Vancouver, Canada to St. Louis alone. It was his first time seeing the national side. He mingled amongst fellow supporters and made friends on match day. In the ecstasy of being amongst his people, he became joyfully intoxicated. He became tearful. He was with his people where he belonged. Someone in this new group of friends took him back to his hotel room after the match as he was in no state to do so on his own. When the man woke up, his wallet and all his personal belongings were next to him on his nightstand. It had been the happiest he had ever been.

Upon returning, I was back to reality. Life would again consist of applying to places, occupying my time with football, watching *Seinfeld* reruns, and feeling useless. Although interviews were had, there was no success. Maybe there was something wrong with my presentation? I certainly had everything I needed on paper. It also could have been differences in culture during the interviews. Maybe I didn't respond with an energetic enough "well!" when I was asked "how are you?" during the introductions. Whatever the reason ended up being, it was depressing to be unemployed.

While on the job hunt, I needed something to feel normal besides football. To take the worry and tension away, I would visit my old professor and friend Dr. Fishman and even sit in his classes that he was teaching at night. His students wondered who I was after randomly just showing up one day and sitting in. While I listened to his lectures, there would be occasions when he would call on me to answer a question. It felt good to feel some normalcy and a state of comfort again for a little while and to distract me from what was going on.

At least I would always have my crutch in the form of football to lean on. I had followed Atlético Madrid closely throughout the season and they were in pole position to do the unlikely and win La Liga. On May 17, 2014, Atleti would face FC Barcelona on the final day of the league at the Camp Nou. Atleti would win the title by win or draw. It turned out to be a card-heavy affair as nine yellows were given throughout the match. Alexis Sánchez put the home side up in the 33rd minute after sending a powerful shot from a very difficult angle from far out past Courtois. It was an unusual goal, and if he would've tried it multiple times after, he probably could not have replicated the goal. Despite Barcelona's lackluster season by their standards, at this point, they would walk away with the title. However, on the other side of half time, in the 49th minute, a corner by the Atleti captain Gabi found the head of Uruguayan hardman Diego Godín who headed into the ground. The ball bounced past the goalkeeper Pinto and into the net. The reaction from myself and my father was the same as when Iniesta scored the winner in the World Cup final four years prior. We wanted the underdog Atlético to win. They worked hard and tirelessly all season to get to this point and a new winner in La Liga kept things fresh. Messi would score for Barcelona about 15 minutes later, but the goal was ruled offside. The clock was ticking, but rooting for Atlético, it felt like the clock moved much, much slower. As the seconds passed, the anxiety remained. However, Atlético Madrid was able to hold out and become champions for the first time since 1996. Even the Barcelona fans applauded

Atlético Madrid's accomplishment. Diego Simeone and his men had taken the La Liga crown from the usuals. The image that stayed with me would be Diego Simeone sitting on the bench after the victory and laughing and smiling to himself.

Atlético's sensational season was not limited to the domestic league. They managed to get to the Champions League final as well. I was hoping they would win that too. The final would be played only a week after their league title-clinching match. And the opposition would be their local rival, Real Madrid. A Madrid derby to determine the champion of Europe for the 2013/2014 season. The match would take place in Lisbon at the Estádio da Luz. Atlético scored yet again through a Godín header in the 33rd minute and remained steadfast in their bunker. Atlético defended and defended. The team was running out of gas and it showed. In the 93rd minute, a Luka Modrić corner would find the head of Sergio Ramos who headed it past Courtois. The goal deflated the Colchoneros. The match went into extra time where Ángel Di María dribbled past three Atleti players and shot at goal. Courtois saved the shot but the rebound went to the far post where Gareth Bale headed it in. Real would score two more from Marcelo and Cristiano Ronaldo, the latter from the penalty spot. It was not going to be a double for Atlético in their great season, but no one expected them to win the league and be in the Champions League final in the first place. It reiterated to me the notion of the underdog having their day, their opportunity to succeed. And that's all I wanted for myself as well, an opportunity. But there weren't any at the moment and I just kept trucking on.

While I was handing resumes out, applying for jobs online, and experiencing an ever-increasing sense of desperation, the World Cup in Brazil rolled around. The land of Ronaldo, Zico, Garrincha, and Pelé. The land of *o jogo bonito*. The land of carnival and sandy beaches. A land with one of the richest footballing traditions. I met a few guys who were football fans on my return to Mobile, and we made it a habit to watch a lot of the matches together. Their focus and support were mostly on the USA matches, but they wanted to watch as many matches as they could during the World Cup.

The US started their campaign against one of their international rivals, Ghana. The guys and I were just getting to the bar, running a few minutes late. The place was packed and we had to stand in line for a table. While standing in line, Clint Dempsey scored for the US in the 1st minute of play. A couple of passes between the US ended up at Dempsey's feet who dribbled past the Ghanian defender and shot past the keeper. The ball hit the inside of the far post and bounced into the net. Chants of "USA! USA!" suddenly exploded at the bar. Ghana tested Tim Howard a few times throughout the match and would find the equalizer in the 82nd minute through André Ayew, son of legendary Ghanian footballer Abedi Pele. Ayew ran into the box, latching onto a pass, and put the ball into the net with the outside of his left boot. The US would get a corner in the 86th minute. Graham Zusi would deliver it and substitute John Anthony Brooks would head the ball into the ground, which bounced past the keeper. Again, the bar exploded with USA chants. Brooks later said in an interview that he dreamt before the game that he would score near the end of regulation. Incredibly, it came true. It was easy to get caught up in the USA fervor at the bar with the rest of the crowd, the country being my place of residence. And the guys and I would do it again for the second group stage game against Cristiano's Portugal six days later. The match took place in Manaus in the Amazon Rainforest in a stadium that was constructed a few years before this World Cup. Portugal came out strong. They were hammered by the Germans in their opening match, conceding four goals. They needed this win and things started excellently for them after a botched clearance ended up at the feet of Nani who fired his cannonball shot past Tim Howard. The US had chances, including a Michael Bradley shot that was cleared near the goal line. They would have to wait until the 64th minute when Jermaine Jones shot from 25 yards out, sending a curler past Beto. The distance, the fact that numerous players were in the way of the goal, and the trajectory of the ball dumbfounded everyone. Beto stood there like he had seen a ghost. This equalizer was epic in proportion. But the US was not done yet. 17 minutes later, the US continued to attack. A cross came to Clint Dempsey who scored the goal with his abdomen. The US looked like they were on the way to their second win, but in the 5th minute of stoppage time, Cristiano sent in a beautiful, pinpoint cross into the box. The ball met the head of Varela. The bullet of a header went past Tim Howard. American hearts were broken and the atmosphere in the sports bar plummeted with our disappointment in the result. However, the US played with spirit, with gusto, and they were to be taken a bit more seriously than their reputation as a nation who isn't great at the beautiful game. Their last match was against Germany. Prior to the match, the US was on a path to go through to the knockout stages, but things weren't official yet. Portugal played Ghana in the other group game. Although Portugal ultimately won, 2-1 and the US lost 0-1 to Germany, the US's goal difference was better than Portugal's, so they moved on to the next phase as group runners-up.

Of course, the other team that I watched with a keen eye was my birth country, Bosnia. This was Bosnia's first appearance at a World Cup. It was very special to me and my family. After not qualifying for any major tournaments since becoming an independent country, they finally qualified after a dramatic qualifying stage. And who better to face than Messi's Argentina in their opener at the famous Maracanã stadium? The match started unluckily for Bosnia. A set-piece delivered into the box by Messi ended up hitting the leg of Sead Kolašinac. The ball diverted into the Bosnian net and Argentina were up 1-0 after only three minutes. Bosnia played quite well in the first half and had chances to equalize, but Chiquito Romero kept them at bay. Messi's first half was somewhat quiet by his standards. Relative unknown, Muhamed Bešić, was tasked with trying to make him as uncomfortable as possible with the help of his Bosnian teammates. But it didn't matter. Messi is inevitable. In the 65th minute, Bešić was attempting to follow a Messi run but a teammate simultaneously tried to stop Messi. The two Bosnians crashed into one another, and Messi found a sliver of space, shooting the ball past Asmir Begović in goal, hitting the post and into the net. It was 2-0 Argentina. Bosnia was deflated. They lost some sense of urgency after that. We knew it was practically over at home. Vedad Ibišević gave Bosnia a small lifeline after sending the ball between Romero's legs in the 85th minute., but it wasn't enough. The match ended 2-1. Bosnia played well considering who the opposition was. The other match in the group was Iran and Nigeria and it finished goalless. So, the situation wasn't terrible for Bosnia. They had an opportunity in the next match against Nigeria. Bosnia would score through Edin Džeko. Or would they? The linesman called offside. Replays show that Džeko was not offside at all. We were obviously angry at this injustice that we had clearly suffered. Džeko would have another opportunity, but the Nigerian keeper made the save. On the other end, Emenike found Peter Odemwingie in the box who tapped it in. There were calls in the buildup to the goal when Emenike was trying to get around Emir Spahić. The latter claimed he had been pushed when the former was going around him. The ref didn't heed the complaints. Bosnia had more chances including Džeko hitting the post near the end of the match. But it was not to be for the Bosnian Diamond and his country. Bosnia crashed out of the World Cup. The win over Iran in the third group stage was a small consolation. Argentina, beating Iran and then Nigeria, would be the group winner with the team from the African continent being runners-up.

Defending champs Spain looked like a shell of their former glorious selves, losing to the Dutch who exacted revenge on their loss in the final in 2010 by putting five goals past the Spaniards. Spain's losing streak continued against Chile in their second match. The country that had dominated the international game for over half a decade failed in the group stage. The glory years for *La Roja* were over.

The hosts, Brazil, qualified with ease in the group stage, winning two matches over Croatia and Cameroon, but drawing with Mexico. They were obviously one of the favorites due to host status. They would face Chile in the round of 16 in a physical and tightly contested match which ultimately went to penalties. However, the Chileans missed three of their five penalties and Brazil missed one less. Brazil was through and would await the winner of Uruguay and Colombia. In the match between the two South American countries, James Rodríguez would score the goal of the tournament and would win the Puskas Award (the award for the best goal given out by FIFA at the annual awards ceremony) for it later on in the year. In the 25th minute, James chested down a header from a teammate and would volley it from roughly 25 yards out. The ball hit the underside of the crossbar and bounced into the goal. It was the most beautiful goal of the tournament in terms of aesthetics. James would end up being the top goal scorer of the tournament with six goals.

The match that had the most personal meaning to me in the round of 16 was between the USA and Belgium. Again, I met with my buddies at the same bar. The Americans' determination and spirit had me invested in this match. The atmosphere at the bar and my buddies' support of the US pulled me in easily. I became part of the herd, a true believer in the American cause for this match. In regulation, Belgium's Kevin De Bruyne ran the show and dominated, but the Americans hung on through Tim Howard's heroic saves. The Americans themselves had a chance to win it in stoppage time. The ball was headed to Chris Wondolowski who was one-on-one with Courtois. However, when he received the ball in what would have been practically a tap-in, he mis-hit it and skied it. In what would surely have been a winner, the US blew their chance. In extra time, Kevin De Bruyne found the breakthrough with a low, but powerful shot past Tim Howard. The Americans were throwing everything up front now to equalize but the Belgians caught them on a counterattack that was finished by Romelu Lukaku. Although it was 2-0, my buddies and I still had a little bit of hope, and we were rewarded. A goal by Julian Green in the 107th minute kept the contest alive. The American optimism had taken ahold of me. The bar echoed with chants of "I believe that we will win!" and, despite my naturally pessimistic character, I believed that the US could still win it. The opportunity to tie the match arrived from a set piece. After a trick play on the set piece, Clint Dempsey was one-on-one with Courtois, but the latter came out very quickly off his line to block Dempsey's attempt. And that was all she wrote. Belgium held on to see the match out. Tim Howard made a record number of saves (16) and kept the US in the match. If it weren't for his saves, Belgium would've easily dispatched the US. He earned himself the nickname Secretary of Defense for his performance. I was disappointed. I hoped for the upset, and it was so close to happening, but the football gods had other ideas.

Brazil versus Colombia was the highlight of the quarterfinal stage. Possession would be about equal; shots on goals were also just about even. However, the difference was in fouls. Brazil committed 31 fouls while Colombia committed 23. However, only two yellow cards were given apiece. The referee was criticized for his performance for not controlling the game. Ultimately Brazil went through after a corner that Thiago Silva tapped into the net at the far post and the second goal from a wonderful freekick from David Luiz. Colombia scored a penalty in the 80th minute. Brazil would win the match but would suffer the loss of Neymar after Juan Carlos Zuniga kneed him in the back close to the end of regulation. Neymar would miss the remainder of the tournament which meant Brazil would be without their talisman against the Germans in the semis. It was a shame to see Colombia and James Rodríguez eliminated as they played attacking football that people enjoyed, and also because they were a fresh face in the latter stages of the tournament. The guys I watched the match with knew that the better team had lost, but that's football.

We gathered again for the very hyped semifinal between the hosts and Germany. Brazilian players held a shirt in support of Neymar due to his injury and unavailability. Personally, I don't think Neymar's presence would've mattered too much. The Germans ripped the Brazilians apart easily. The 2nd and 3rd goal scored by the Germans wowed and shocked us in how quick of a succession it happened. Once the Germans piled on even further, shock became laughter and laughter turned into incredulity at the final whistle. No one expected the Germans to destroy Brazil 7-1 in their home country. The hosts were embarrassed, and Brazilians didn't know whether to cry, laugh, or be angry at their own team. Brazil's foe, Argentina, sang *Brazil, decime que se siente* (Brazil, tell me how it feels?) enjoying the misery their rivals and neighbors suffered at the hands of Germany. The song is sung to the tune of Creedence Clearwater Revival's *Bad Moon Rising*. The original lyrics reference Argentina's goal against Brazil in the 1990 World Cup, orchestrated by Maradona and scored by Caniggia and that Maradona is better than Pelé. Argentina fans sang this throughout the tournament but after the Germans shellacked their neighbors 7-1, the lyrics were changed referencing the goals conceded by Brazil and that the score won't be forgotten over the years and of Brazil's support of all the teams that

Argentina played at the current World Cup. It was classic football banter.

Argentina's route to the final was a laborious one. A goal in the 118th minute by Di María assisted by the magic man, Lionel Messi himself, would beat Switzerland in the round of 16. Although the Swiss had a chance after the goal, the post was Argentina's friend, and they moved onto the quarters to face Belgium. Against Belgium, a moment of spontaneity and creativity by Gonzalo Higuaín in the 8th minute would prove decisive. An intended pass for another teammate hit a Belgian player. Higuaín struck the ball at half-volley past a helpless Courtois, and this would be the point of difference. They faced the Dutch in the semifinals where the match went to a penalty shootout. Here, the hero would be Sergio "Chiquito" Romero. He would save Ron Vlaar and Wesley Sneijder's penalties. Argentina would convert all of theirs. They booked themselves a ticket to the final against their familiar football foe, Germany. However, watching Argentina play, something was amiss. What appeared to be Argentina's issue? Was the opposition difficult? Were they battling themselves mentally? Was the pressure too much for Messi and his teammates? Were they not as talented as we had thought? In my opinion, while the teams that they faced were not pushovers, as made evident by their respective performances against the Albiceleste, Argentina lacked the offensive chemistry to produce more. It was Messi who had to marshal the midfield and facilitate the offense almost on his own with the assistance of Di María. Without the necessary help in midfield like he would have at the World Cup in Qatar in 2022, it truly was a grand achievement to almost single-handedly drag this side to the final.

I went to the same sports bar as before. A few Germans also congregated on the other side of the bar as well, but no Argentina supporters in sight. This would be the third final of a World Cup where Argentina faced Germany for eternal glory. In 1986, Argentina won 3-2. In 1990, Germany won 1-0. With a little less than 25 minutes played, a golden opportunity presented itself for Argentina. A misplaced back header by the Germans ended up at the feet of Gonzalo Higuaín. He was one-on-one with Neuer but decided to shoot from the top of box, slicing the ball, which would go wide of goal. Later in the first half, Higuaín seemed to have redeemed himself after he tapped in a cross from Lavezzi. He began celebrating like a madman, but the linesman correctly ruled the goal offside. In the 33rd minute, Benedikt Höwedes fouled Pablo Zabaleta with his studs high up, catching the Argentinian on his inner thigh. The German received a yellow for his infraction, but it could've, and some argue, should've been a red. A couple of minutes later, André Schürrle tested Romero on the other side. Argentina were the more adventurous team in the first half, finding room in the final third but not being able to find the final touch. On the other side of half time, within two minutes, the little magician himself, Messi, had a great opportunity to score, coming from the left side of the box. He hit the ball with his preferred foot, beating Neuer in the process, but the ball went slightly wide of the far post. In the 56th minute, Higuaín received a ball over the top and ran towards the right side of the box and Neuer came out to meet him. Neuer clashed into Higuaín knee-first into the head while attempting to punch the ball. The ref somehow decided that Higuaín fouled Neuer instead of the other way around and it was Germany's ball. I couldn't believe it. Had it been the other way around, Neuer most likely would've been sent off. There were half-chances for both sides in the rest of the second half but nothing that troubled either keeper. Extra-time was here just like it had been in the World Cup finals two editions prior. Not a minute in the first period of extra time, Schürrle had a shot on goal from a short distance, but Romero parried the ball away. A few minutes later, on the other end, a cross into the German box found Rodrigo Palacio who tried to lob the ball over Manuel Neuer into the net, but the ball went wide. In the 113th minute, the decisive goal would come for the Germans. Andre Schürrle was on the wing and crossed the ball to substitute Mario Götze, who chested it and volleyed it past Sergio Romero, who guessed the wrong way. This made Germany four-time World Cup champions. Sounds of jubilation from the Germans, visions of tears and sadness from the Argentinians. Argentina's third World Cup was not to be and Messi's reputation with Argentina, whether deserved or not, took a hit. Although he won the Golden Ball for being the best player of the tournament, he was unable to carry Argentina to victory. Of course, Messi would bear a lot of criticism which typically included that he couldn't win the big one without his Barcelona teammates and that he would never be on equal footing with Maradona in Argentina and that lastly he just wasn't good enough to lift the World Cup trophy. It was sad to see such a wonderful player receive such bashing after dragging Argentina to the final. At the time, it wasn't unreasonable to think that this was it for him in terms of opportunities to win the World Cup.

After the tournament had ended and my beautiful distraction was gone, I went back to just continuing sending resumes out and contacting potential employers. In my mind, there was nothing else I could do. And finally, FINALLY, a few days after the World Cup ended, on the way home from one of those trips around town handing out resumes, my phone rang. It was a company in west Mississippi calling me, wanting to interview me. Within a week I interviewed. I drove over which nearly took an hour and a half. After it had concluded, they told me to call Friday the week after. I couldn't wait for next Friday. When it finally got here, I must've called four or five times as my anxiousness and eagerness got the best of me. I was clearly showing signs of desperation. I had been in search of a job for about a year. I finally got a hold of the hiring manager, and he offered me a position. The job search was over. It was a relief, a burden off my shoulders, and I could breathe again.

CHAPTER 10

Hometown Heroes

When the Saints Go Marching In

After finally finding employment after the World Cup in 2014, the next step in my life was happenstance. I found romance in the fall of 2014 after I met my future wife at an American football game that we both attended. I noticed her standing in the row below me, almost directly in front of me. She was literally under my nose. It seemed fated. We got to talking, one thing followed another, and we ended up dating. We ultimately got engaged two years and a few months later. During all of this, I ended up finding employment back in Mobile so I could be closer with my family and her. All the pieces were falling together for me.

While these years went on, a little something was still missing. Once these aforementioned needs were met, being part of a community of like-minded football people and supporting a local team shot to the top of the priority list. We decided to give it a shot with the team at the university I had attended.

Obviously, I could not expect high quality football considering the level, but I hoped to at least find myself somehow in the team since they represented my alma mater. We attended for a few seasons and made acquaintances with a few of the players and staff. We tried to imitate the chants from English football terraces. We even traveled to games that were over 6 hours away by car. However, our attempts to mimic the style of football terraces in England fell on deaf ears. A decent portion of the crowd were parents of the players. The other half were students in attendance. Our creativity did not reach their imaginations. They were used to "Defense, Defense!" and "Let's Go [insert team name here]." I could not exactly put my finger as to why that happened. Were they afraid to express themselves? It could not have been not knowing the words to the chants, as we made chant sheets and passed them around. Maybe they were not accustomed to intense participation by supporters and were only used to being mostly spectators? Or were they accustomed to the general American fan culture? We tried to raise the atmosphere levels, to lead those people out of the cave and introduce them to football culture that is prevalent around the world, to make our environment a product of us, but when it was only us two, we failed. Coupled with this personal defeat and the acquaintances we made graduating or moving on to other places, we had to find our desired community somewhere else.

Luckily for us, the game was growing and growing on a local and national scale. It was getting more popular due to the world being more connected than ever and numerous leagues being available on streaming platforms. And with the sport increasing in popularity, a local team popped up called AFC Mobile, nicknamed the Azaleas (due to the prevalence of the flowering shrub in the area). The team was founded in 2015, but it did not start competing in a league until 2017. The club's set up involved a board with a small group of private owners. Individuals like Abram Chamberlain, Patrick Dungan, and several others in the administration and management were instrumental in founding the club and running it on a day-to-day basis, including on match days, whether that meant helping set up things around the stadium, taking photos, doing the announcing for the match, or selling merchandise. The board members cared and they devoted an incredible amount of time to the club while having families and careers. Once the club had the infrastructure in place, it began its journey in the Gulf Coast Premier League. And with each club in the world having their ultras, barras bravas, torcidas, whatever word you fancy, AFC Mobile's supporters' group was called the Causeway Rebellion. The name came about as the causeway is a landmark road in

Mobile that connects it with Baldwin County, which is on the eastern shore of Mobile Bay. The other part of the name indicates that the group shows grit and a determination to be seen and heard for their cause, which is supporting AFC Mobile to the nth degree. Two of the founders of the group were Keath Kaufmann, a Chicago transplant to Mobile and Michael Shartava, a Russian émigré to the United States since 1991. This group was formed in the 11th hour. They invited their colleagues and friends to the matches. They found themselves a section in the stands at "The Lip" (the nickname for Archbishop Lipscomb Stadium where Mobile would play their home matches), where they planted their custom flags and hung their banners. They brought drums and their voices. Some of them brought their little children. Although the group consisted of somewhere between 20 and 25 regular members, they created such an atmosphere that it sounded three times the physical number. The creative chants were a huge shock at the matches in AFC Mobile's inaugural season as they diverted from the uninspiring and tedious "Let's go [insert team name]" and "Defense! Defense!"

We heard about this new team in town and decided to check it out. We were shocked by what we had discovered. This seemed a lot different than we were accustomed to seeing at the university. The group replicated a smaller-sized version of the atmosphere one would expect to see in the German Bundesliga and the English Premier League. From that first match we attended, we were hooked. We ended up making friends and acquaintances over time with members of the Causeway Rebellion and would become part of it ourselves.

For a few members of the Rebellion, matchday began shortly after sunrise. The faithful would gather at Joe Cain's grave at Church Street Graveyard. Joe Cain is the innovator of the modern observance of Mardi Gras, which originally started in Mobile. Here, these believers would read a poem and have an alcoholic beverage and toast Mobile's very well renowned misfit. Mardi Gras is arguably the biggest holiday for Mobile. It is a party lasting over a month, with a full schedule of parades, balls, and general revelry. The crescendo of the Mardi Gras season begins with Joe Cain Day, the Sunday before Fat Tuesday. It is the American equivalent to carnival, with parades, masks, costumes, parties, etc. all being part of it. As the Rebellion deems themselves misfits, it was appropriate to make Joe Cain the patron saint of the group.

For those not participating in the morning rituals, the typical day of a home match started at Lucky Irish Pub & Grill, a bar less than two miles from the Lip. Through his connections with the management, Kaufmann convinced them to make Lucky the official pre-match meeting ground for the Causeway Rebellion.

Lucky was more than accommodating and also offered matchday specials on food and drinks. Moreover, on occasion when Mobile's matches are a far traveling distance this pub allowed the Causeway Rebellion and other supporters to meet there and stream the matches, creating a raucous atmosphere to cheer the team on. As the pre-match pub group put in their last calls, the southern tradition of tailgating was under way in the parking lot of the Lip. Dedicated members of the Causeway Rebellion, Dustin Wilson and Kenny Powell, started the tailgate by setting up tents, lighting the grill, and putting out coolers of drinks that drew the rest of the group from Lucky. It took a true trooper to tailgate in the fully exposed parking lot, as the sun in Mobile is merciless in the late spring and summer when the matches would take place. About 30 to 45 minutes prior to kickoff, the group would assemble inside the gate to get ready for the march to their turf. This march would pass in front of all the home and away fans and is a spectacle for all the senses. For the ears, it is an euphonic sound of drums, tambourines, cowbell, the occasional horn, the rustling clink of Mardi Gras beads, and the voices of the faithful. For the nose, it is a smell of sulfur emanating from the colorful flares that are lit at the beginning of the march. For the eyes, it is flags waving in unison and the lock step march of dozens of individuals in AFC Mobile colors. They would take their places and the concert would begin for the next two hours. Chant and song sheets would make the rounds for those interested in being more than just a spectator. These amateur musicians would remain steady for 90+ minutes with their vocals and instruments. Agitation of the opposing team's players is also quite common. Although the number of Rebellion members is usually smaller at away matches (depending on the distance to the other team's ground), the intensity and passion did not change.

All of this fanaticism was not for naught. A perfect example of the Causeway Rebellion's influence on a match took place in an away match to Pensacola FC on June 16, 2018. Due to the close distance between the two cities, a decent number of the members made the trip to the Sunshine State. Unfortunately, the match did not start out great for the Azaleas. AFC Mobile was down 3-0 a few minutes in the second half. Mobile managed to nick a goal and made it 3-1. While the Causeway Rebellion was down in spirit with the score, they were active in the flesh. The drums kept beating, the chants kept going, and the banter continued with opposing players. Naturally, the banter with the opposing players is to distract them and make them lose focus in the match. One of those players had enough; when the ball rolled out for a throw-in, he kicked it into the crowd and hit one of the Rebellion members in the face. Big mistake. This awoke a sleeping giant; the spirit of the Causeway Rebellion was renewed. The sound of the Causeway increased. The Mobile players felt it as the sounds reenergized them as well and it showed in the scoreline. 3-2 in the 84th minute, 3-3 in the 85th minute, and 3-4 in the 86th minute due to a beautifully curled shot by striker and club legend, Chisom Ogbonna. Ogbonna ran his way over to the Causeway Rebellion section and slid on his knees, pointing to the heavens, perhaps grateful that he just completed the comeback for his club and made a group of hardcore supporters animalistically roar in joy like they had not roared before. These were sounds made from the depth of the soul. Mobile held on and won. One of the club captains, Memo Lumbreras, jumped amongst the supporters, who embraced him while he raised his fist in the air in victory. Club officials and players all agree that the Causeway Rebellion's sounds and palpable energy pushed the Azaleas to victory in the match against Pensacola and became one of its, if not the most, memorable matches.

As to the players who were probably most identified with AFC Mobile, two immediately spring to mind: Memo Lumbreras and Pensacola match-winner Chisom Ogbonna. Lumbreras became a legendary figure at the club, as he became one of the captains after making the team, then began volunteering to help and assist the club on matchdays, which included cleaning the pitch and stadiums, packing boxes and supplies and loading them into vehicles. Lumbreras' loyalty, dedication, and longevity with the club moved him into bigger roles and responsibilities. As a center-back, he would marshal the backline. He was a no-nonsense defender. Once he retired as a player in 2019, further opportunities appeared to remain involved with the club on a volunteer basis. However, that didn't last long. One of the previous shareholders sold his stake to Lumbreras and the AFC Mobile board approved the sale, making Lumbreras part-owner. Months later, Lumbreras became the Director of Coaching for U3-U8 and coaching a competitive team for the newly formed AFC Mobile Youth Academy. He was the soul of the team.

Chisom Ogbonna too became a club legend with his goals. He ultimately would become joint top-scorer in the club's history and would give his all on the pitch for Mobile. When he had the ball in the attacking third, you always had the feeling that something could happen to get the ball into the net, whether it was some of his trickery that would get him past an opponent to set up a goal or score one himself. After matches, he would always swing by the supporters' section and thank us with a big, bright, infectious smile. If Lumbreras was the soul of the team, Ogbonna was the heart of it.

We were not only shocked with the existence of the Causeway Rebellion, but we were also shocked with the attendance figures. We expected maybe a couple of hundred people to show, as soccer was not on the top of the sports hierarchy in the American South (despite its popularity as a sport for smaller children). But the attendance figures were quite high within this context. There were times when home matches would draw 1600 people. AFC was easily outdrawing the entire league and even some leagues above the Gulf Coast Premier League. Local politicians would also get invited to do the coin-toss or address the crowd and would be treated like guests of honor. Due to the rise in popularity of the sport, on a national and local level, one of the local politicians, Connie Hudson was the linchpin in getting a brand-new soccer complex built in the Mobile area. The game was growing, there was a community need for it, and Hudson responded by spearheading its construction.

We would travel to several away matches that were within a reasonable distance from Mobile. Other more dedicated members of the Rebellion would travel even farther distances, including to places like Jacksonville, Florida, or Chattanooga, Tennessee, which were roughly six hours away. And things were good for a while. I thought I had found the community that I craved. Unfortunately, the longer I was part of it, the more and more I realized that I saw football differently than the rest of the members of the Rebellion. Although we supported the same team, I was different culturally, on a personal level and a football level than they were. My enthusiasm for being part of it just waned over time. I would still attend matches and support the team, but my participation level severely dropped off. I enjoyed it for a while, but my cultural needs were different and I was back on my imaginary horse on a journey to finding a community that I saw myself reflected in.

During my honeymoon period with AFC Mobile, there was the little matter of the World Cup that was on the horizon. The 2018 edition was held in Russia. It was the first World Cup in an Eastern European country. France were the favorites with quality in every position plus a very deep bench. The other typical powerhouses were in the conversation, but France was the clear one standing out.

My personal opener turned out to be the Iberian Derby in a clash in Group B. Portugal was the most recently crowned European champion in 2016. Spain was trying to restart a new era of their own after the disaster in Brazil in 2014. It was a hot and sunny Friday afternoon. We met up with a few people at a local bar to watch. Upon arrival, the bar manager seemed a bit irked that we requested to watch soccer on the television. He turned the channel for us, but you could tell by body language and his facial expression that this guy seemed to have a dislike for the beautiful game. The match itself turned out to be highly entertaining. Portugal took the lead in the 4th minute through a Cristiano penalty, but Spain answered through Diego Costa in the 24th. Another trading of goals occurred in the 44th and 55th minute respectively. Cristiano's second goal was a howler by Spanish keeper David de Gea whose inability to stop a rather simple shot at him and letting the ball bounce off his hands into the net was reminiscent of Robert Green's at the 2010 World Cup. Spain's answer in the 55th minute was through a set piece that required Diego Costa to tap in the final ball. Finally, Spain would take the lead in the 58th minute through a beautiful bullet of a strike by Nacho Fernández from outside of the box. However, the man of the hour would be Cristiano Ronaldo. In the 88th minute, he struck a free kick past a flatfooted David de Gea and completed his World Cup hattrick. The match would finish 3-3.

For those who buy into the Messi/Cristiano rivalry, the question was how he and Argentina would respond in their opener. Argentina was coached by Jorge Sampaoli, who was appointed as coach in May 2017. Argentina actually struggled to qualify for the World Cup. However, Messi's hattrick in the qualifiers against Ecuador assured qualification. In their World Cup opener, Argentina ran into Iceland's golden generation in the opener and drew 1-1. Argentina didn't look like themselves. Sampaoli's various lineups and numerous players that he constantly experimented with, plus a poor defense, were indicative of a man who had no idea who his best players were nor what his best formation and line up were for optimal success. And Argentina would be exposed in the next match by the tournament's Cinderella story, Croatia. One could say that this was Croatia's second golden generation, after their 3rd place finish in 1998. Led by the diminutive midfield maestro, Luka Modrić, his two partners in midfield, Marcelo Brozović and Ivan Rakitić, a front line of Mario Mandžukić and Ivan Perišić, and a solid defense of Dejan Lovren and Domagoj Vida, Croatia diced and sliced Argentina apart. After a serious error by Willy Caballero where he failed to clear the ball properly, Ante Rebić caught the ball on a volley and struck it into the net. In the 80th minute, Modrić scored with a curling rocket past Caballero. Rakitić scored the 3rd in stoppage time – it was the cherry on top. The world took notice of Croatia after this victory. With this win, Croatia qualified for the Round of 16. Argentina on the other hand was on the brink of elimination. In the last round of group stage matches, they faced Nigeria, whose prospect of going to the next stage was better at that point than the Albiceleste's.

Messi scored in the 14th minute after receiving a long pass from midfield. His first touch was with his thigh, then his left foot which he played a few yards forward for the third and final touch which was the shot that ended up in the back of the net. It was poetry by La Pulga. Argentina now had serious hope to move on, but in the 51st minute disaster struck. Mascherano tussled with an opposition player during a corner and brought him down by wrapping his arms around him. A penalty was given, and Victor Moses coolly dispatched it past Franco Armani. Argentina needed a goal, and it was better late than never. In the 86th minute, Gabriel Mercado sent in a cross; centerback Marcos Rojo was now up front. Mercado found him and the ball ended up at Rojo's feet, who, with his first touch, hit the ball into the bottom corner past Francis Uzoho. The match finished 2-1. In the other group stage match, Iceland lost to Croatia by the same scoreline. This ensured that Argentina would go on to the next round as second place finishers in the group.

Squeezing through to the knockout stages, Argentina would face the favorite, France. This was the marquee match of the round, and it did not disappoint. In the 8th minute, teenage sensation Kylian Mbappé was brought down near the box, and the French would have their first chance. Antoine Griezmann stood over the ball and got it up over the wall. Armani stood in his tracks, ball-watching, but the ball hit the crossbar. Mbappé would trouble the Argentinian defense two minutes later. His speed caused trouble for Marcos Rojo, who brought the teenager down in the box. Penalty for the French. Up steps Griezmann, who calmly slots the ball past Armani, who went the wrong way. It would take a while for Argentina to truly threaten Lloris's goal, but in the 41st minute, the equalizer happened. Ángel Di María from so far out sent a banger near the top corner past the French keeper. The cameras showed a jubilant Maradona celebrating in his box in the stadium. On the other side of half time, Argentina would score again. A Messi shot towards the goal was deflected by Gabriel Mercado past Hugo Lloris. Had Argentina found their groove finally?! The answer was, unfortunately, no. A Pavard wonderstrike, similar to the goal that Nacho Fernández scored against Portugal in the group stage, would even the match at 2-2. Quick foot work and a powerful, low shot by Mbappé that Armani couldn't keep out put the French into the lead in the 64th minute. Only four minutes later, the teenager would complete his brace on a counterattack, using his lightning quick pace, latching on to a ball from target-man Olivier Giroud, striking the ball past Armani. It was 4-2 for Les Bleus and Argentina had to climb a mountain to get back into the match. Time was ticking. Messi got past several French defenders in less than ten minutes from end of regulation but ended up off balance and sent a weak shot towards goal that Lloris had no trouble saving. Three minutes into stoppage time, Messi found Agüero in the box who headed it past Lloris. A couple of more waves of attack by Argentina threatened the French goal, but the match ended 4-3. It was over. Argentina went home. Speculation arose that it would be Messi's last World Cup. Was this it? Would arguably the greatest player of all time not win a World Cup? Would he want to continue to try again four and a half years later? Could he continue? These questions were in everyone's mind at the time of Argentina's elimination, but answers would come in due time.

For those who were keenly intrigued by the Messi/Cristiano debate, the latter also suffered the same destiny as Messi in the Round of 16. Uruguay would knock out Portugal 2-1 only a few hours after Argentina's fate had been sealed. The two superstar players were out.

Being enthralled by Croatia in the group stages, there was no doubt at this point what my focus would be on. Their round of 16 opponent was Denmark. We were invited to a large cookout hosted by a member from the Causeway Rebellion, so I watched the match with some people I knew and others I didn't. I found myself slightly out of my element since the people I didn't know weren't there for the match at all. Anyway, once the match kicked off, I was glued to the screen. And it didn't take long for something to happen. After a very long throw-in into the box in the very first minute by Denmark, the ball found itself at the feet of Mathias Jørgensen. He shot it towards Croatian keeper, Danijel Subašić. He blocked it but the rebound rolled into the net. The Danes were ahead but not for long at all. Three minutes later, after the ball seemed to ping-pong in the Danish penalty box, the ball bounced to Mario Mandžukić who kicked the ball into the net past Kasper Schmeichel. This quick equalizer ended with me letting out a resounding "YES!" to the consternation of the guests who were only there for the barbeque. The match would remain 1-1 in regulation, although Croatia had a few decent chances. In extra time, Croatia's biggest chance to take the lead presented itself when Luka Modrić played a through-ball to Ante Rebić. He rounded Schmeichel but was brought down from behind. Penalty to Croatia! It was time to wrap this match up. Luka Modrić, the little wizard, the playmaker, the man whose grandfather was killed during the Yugoslav Wars in the early 1990s, the man whose family were forced to flee their home because of the war and seek refuge in hotels for years in Croatia during the fighting, stepped up to the spot. Schmeichel guessed right and saved the penalty. I was in disbelief! I was afraid that this was going to have a negative effect on the rest of the players. The match went to penalties, and a hero between the sticks would emerge. Danijel Subašić, the goalkeeper, whose family home was also destroyed during the war, would face Christian Eriksen first. Eriksen went to Subašić's right and the latter got a touch on the ball, which hit the post. At this point, with the tension ratcheted up to the breaking point, I am yelling and screaming expletives and words of encouragement in Serbo-Croatian for every penalty... at my buddy's house with alarmed strangers all around. I was in my own little world of football passion. Croatia would miss the first penalty as well. The next two by each team would be converted. Subašić would save Schöne's penalty, but Schmeichel would save the penalty by Pivarić. We were on the 5th round of penalties. Jørgensen, though not the one who scored the goal in the opening minute of the match, stepped up and sent the ball almost straight down the middle, but Subašić stopped it with his foot. Ivan Rakitić, whose family left Croatia before the war broke out and made their home in Switzerland where he was born, made the very long walk from midfield to the penalty spot, looking straight ahead with his green eyes appearing not to blink at all during the walk up. He looked confident. Schmeichel would try to play mind-games with him by pointing to the spot where Rakitić would place the ball. And Schmeichel was correct in that regard; Rakitić placed it low and powerful to the goalkeeper's right, but Schmeichel would dive to his left. Croatia was through to the quarterfinals and I was elated! I have always hoped that the former Balkan countries would do well. The half-Croat in me and Balkan country supporter was caught up in the fervor and zeitgeist more and more by each match. The passion and intensity would increase. I was captivated by the whole event and Croatia's path and would annoy my significant other by constantly playing songs of national importance.

In the quarters, Croatia faced their northern Slavic cousins, the host country, in a similar match as when they faced Denmark. The Russians scored through a beautifully curled, left-footed wonderstrike by Denis Cheryshev from far outside of the box. It left Subašić stunned in goal., but it wouldn't take long for Croatia to respond. Within ten minutes, Mandžukić crossed the ball into the center of the box, where Andrej Kramarić moved his head downwards and connected with the ball. The ball hit the ground and bounced past Igor Akinfeev. In the 60th minute, Croatia had a chance to go up. A cross into the Russian danger zone caused confusion among the defenders. Ivan Perišić found space and struck the ball, but it hit the inside of the post and rolled parallel to the goal line for a corner. After both sides failed to find a goal in regulation, the match went into extra time. Croatia struck first, through a corner with centerback Domagoj Vida; the Russians would answer in the 115th minute, with a corner goal of their own, when Brazilian born, naturalized Russian citizen, Mário Fernandes, scored a header. The match ended 2-2 in extra time, and another penalty shoot-out for Croatia would be on the agenda. Subašić saved Smolov's first penalty, Croatia would convert their first one through Marcelo Brozović. Russia got on the scoreboard in the second round of penalty kicks, and Kovačić had his saved, so things were back to even. Up stepped Mário Fernandes, but he could not put it in the back of the net, and his shot went wide of the goal. Both teams converted the remaining rounds of the "kicks from the spot" as my referee buddy insists on calling them. Ivan Rakitić, like he did against Denmark, clinched it for Croatia. Croatia were heading to their first World Cup semifinal since 1998.

In the semifinal, Croatia would meet England. The English finished runners-up in a group that included Belgium, Tunisia, and Panama. They beat Colombia in a penalty shoot-out in the round of 16 and Sweden in the quarterfinals. England's fans were singing "Three Lions" or otherwise known as "It's Coming Home" throughout the tournament. "It" referring to the World Cup, and "home" referring to England as the country that established the modern-day version of the game. Whether the English fans sang it with humor or actual sincerity, it didn't matter to the Croatians. They didn't need more motivation for the semifinal. The country of Croatia and the flag was enough to motivate them. In addition, there was a certain sense of brotherhood amongst the Croatian players. Some players' families left Croatia because of the conflict in the Balkans, others moved to different cities in Croatia where the situation was not as bad. Players like Ivan Rakitić weren't even born in Croatia. Others like Dejan Lovren were born in Bosnia to Bosnian-Croat parents and moved to Germany because of being displaced due to the war. There was a real sense of camaraderie amongst them, to give everything for Croatia. This was visible on the pitch and even before the start of matches, during the playing of the national anthems. They sang from their hearts and with passion in their chests.

I looked forward to this match quite a bit. During the tournament, it seems the world and time itself stands still. It is difficult to focus on anything else, especially when the country that you have a connection to is doing well and progressing in the tournament. On the day of the semi-final, I was in an important work meeting. Luckily it ended sooner than I expected, and I hastily packed my belongings up to catch the match. One of my colleagues knew about the match and stated to me in all sincerity "I know what's important." I bolted out of there like a bat out of hell and drove to my parents' house.

It was a tense match, and my dad and I were both on the edge of our seats. Trippier scored from a free kick for England in the 5th minute. In the 30th minute, the great forward, Harry Kane, had a golden opportunity to double England's lead, but Subašić saved the first shot and the rebound. The game went on and on and with every minute the nervousness increased. Was Croatia ever going to score? Yes, they were. Ivan Perišić from a Vrsaljko cross hit the ball with the side of his boot past goalkeeper Jordan Pickford. 1-1. Four minutes later, Perišić's shot would hit the post; it surely looked like it was going in and I jumped from the couch letting out a long "ooh!". I kept tapping my foot anxiously against the floorboard. The referee blew the whistle at the end of regulation and the match went into extra time. At this point, my mother came home and all three of us were glued to the TV. In extra time, England's chance came when John Stones headed the ball from a corner. It was too reminiscent of Russia's second goal against Croatia, but the Croatians learned from their mistake and had an additional player near that post. The ball was cleared off the line. Then the moment came in the 109th minute. A Croatian cross was blocked. However, the clearance ended up in the air, and Perišić headed the ball towards the danger area. John Stones, not paying attention, did not see Mandžukić sneak in behind. With his left foot, Mandžukić shot the ball into the right side of the goal, past Pickford. The household exploded with jubilant celebration. High fives and yelling all around. Ten more minutes of tension couldn't dampen our elation as Croatia saw the game out. Croatia, a country of less than 4 million people, was going to the World Cup final.

Croatia would face favorites France in the final. This World Cup was the first and only one, so far, where the whole family watched it together. No doubt it had to do with Croatia being in the final. The togetherness was tinged with alienation, the sense of both being grounded in the city where we made our home, while feeling this strong connection to a country that was part of Yugoslavia and that is thousands of miles away. We ended up all wearing jerseys of Zlatan Ibrahimović, each of us wearing a shirt from a different team that Zlatan played for. We were part of the Balkan diaspora, and the matching kits were another bit of symbolism – as different as the shirts were from each other, they were all Zlatan and we made a colorful yet cohesive group. Zlatan was a piece of the Balkan diaspora as well. For those of us who watched the match around the world, who weren't living in the former Yugoslavia anymore, we had this one moment of connectedness as we all hoped and prayed for this team to prove themselves in the biggest way on the international stage. I woke up incredibly nervous before the final. A local restaurant opened earlier than normal for the match, so we went there. They did not expect a full house, but even before the doors were unlocked, there was a small crowd waiting to enter. To my own surprise, it was packed to the rafters before kickoff, and some people stood near the bar. The match started in relative silence, or as much silence as can be achieved in a room full of thirsty football fans arguing with the waitresses about Alabama blue laws. Blue laws in "the land of the free" are intended to restrict sinful activities such as drinking before 10:00 am. Since 10 o'clock happened to also be the kickoff time, there was a sudden rush for everyone to put in their beer orders and attention to the match was questionable. The French took the lead in the 18th minute. After a highly dubious foul on Antoine Griezmann was called, he delivered a free-kick into Croatia's box. Mario Mandžukić would accidentally flick it into his own net and the French were leading. The response from the restaurant's crowd was quiet. I didn't know if it this was because they were rooting for Croatia or whether this was going to be the standard bar crowd. However, I would have my answer soon, as the *Vatreni* quickly responded. After a ball to the wing by Luka Modrić, the ball bounced onto several Croatian players' heads. Vida laid it off to Perišić who took a couple of touches then sent a rocket through the crowd of defenders, past Hugo Lloris. The restaurant exploded. I couldn't believe the restaurant crowd's response to this. It turned out to be a very heavily pro-Croatia crowd. Ten minutes later, another controversy. A corner by the French found the head of Matuidi, who headed it towards goal; Perišić who was marking Matuidi was close to him. Matuidi headed it onto Perišić's extended hand while the latter was also in the air. After reviewing the call, a penalty was awarded to France and Griezmann dispatched it. Shortly after half-time Rebić tested Lloris and the goalkeeper tipped it over the bar. The French would score through Paul Pogba in the 59th minute. His initial shot was blocked but his follow up left Subašić flat footed and allowed the ball to hit the net without resistance. The French piled on as the starlet Mbappé would extend France's lead further after a low, but powerful shot from outside of the box. I still had hope, perhaps misplaced. The French were leading 4-1 with almost thirty minutes to go. Four minutes later, Mandžukić was pressing Lloris when the latter received the ball. A Lloris blunder allowed Mandžukić to kick the ball into the net. There was a little lifeline left. A later shot by Rakitić went wide of the goal. And that was all she wrote. France were champions for the second time in their history. Despite what I thought were two unjust calls that led to two goals by France and in addition, Croatia's fatigue for playing their previous knockout matches all the way to penalties, the French were a high-quality side who were deserved winners. Of course I wanted Croatia to win, but football is like life, you don't always get what you want. I was disappointed, like someone had punched me in the gut or like I had suffered my first breakup. However I will say, no one expected Croatia to get as far as the final and they could go home holding their heads high. And I, too, had to move on from the defeat and look towards the future. In terms of emotional involvement, this had been probably my favorite World Cup but the football gods had bigger plans for aficionados and romantics like me at the next one in Qatar, a four and a half year wait. In the meantime, we had a wedding to plan.

CHAPTER 11

There and Back Again

Come Fly with Me

In the latter half of 2018, planning for our wedding would begin. We settled for a spring date as anything in the fall would compete with college football, the summer would be too hot and humid, and the winter would not be a good fit.

When it was time to send wedding invitations out, Dr. Fishman and his wife were of course on the list. I wanted my highly influential mentor, my dear friend, to be present at one of the most important days of my life. I kept in touch with Dr. Fishman after he retired over the years and even after he moved away to be closer to his grandchildren. After his move, he endured a nasty fall that split his head open and fractured two of his vertebrae. He was in and out of hospitals. Three months before the wedding, I emailed him to ask for his address to send the invitation to him and his wife. With him still not back to his best, I didn't expect him to make it but nonetheless, I wanted to send him an invitation as a symbolic and friendly gesture. He emailed me back and off the invitation went into the mailbox. I hoped that he would make it. The wedding would not be complete without him. Unfortunately, it was not to be a perfect wedding. A month later, I received a text message from a former classmate who also had taken Dr. Fishman's classes. The text message hit me in my chest like an 18-wheeler while simultaneously yanking a piece of my heart out in the process. The former classmate informed me that Fishman had passed away a few days earlier. I was devastated. I just stopped working and cried. The man who woke me up out of my autopilot life, who guided me and gave me a meaningful sense of direction, was dead. I mourned and expressed my condolences to his adult children and his wife. It took me several days to return to a sense of normalcy.

After months and months of planning and help from family members and friends, the wedding day was finally here. My brother from another mother, Juliano, flew in from Brazil as I chose him to be the best man. Others came from different states to be present. As you can guess, our wedding incorporated certain things from football. We danced to "You'll Never Walk Alone," a staple sung by the Dortmund faithful as well as fans of a few other clubs in Europe. After completing the vows and our first kiss as a married couple, we held up a custom-made scarf donning blue and yellow with DEDIĆ UNITED in big letters.

As we walked out of the venue, instead of throwing rice or birdseed at us, our dear friends lit flares in celebration. It was fantastic.

Two weeks later, we went on our honeymoon to England, Germany, Austria, and Croatia. This was not our first choice. We initially planned for New Zealand as we wanted to experience the land where the *Lord of the Rings* movies were filmed. But a very long prospective plane flight to New Zealand and the pull of being finally able to watch several football matches in Europe was too much. The scale was heavily tilted towards the Old Continent.

In England, we visited the great city by the sea, Portsmouth. Why did we visit Portsmouth? When my significant other started following the beautiful game on a serious and regular basis, she wanted to pick a club that was of her own choosing and not influenced by me. She had an affinity for England due to her being enamored with English culture. However, she did not want to pick a top six team so as not to appear like a "plastic" fan. She actually didn't pick any club in the English Premier League, or the Championship, or League One. She picked Pompey out of League 2 after she learned all of their players' names while playing with the club in a "from the bottom to the top" career mode in the FIFA 14 video game. As a result of her familiarity with the digital characters, she began following their real-life counterparts. Our honeymoon was sort of planned around football. Portsmouth vs. Coventry City was going to be my first match abroad and my first match in England.

On April 21, 2019, we arrived in Portsmouth absolutely jet lagged from our flight. A nap was in order. Afterwards, fish and chips for dinner at a small restaurant down the street would be our first taste of traditional English food. The next morning, we walked downstairs and enjoyed a full English breakfast in the quaint in-house dining room. We only intended to eat a normal amount, in order to enjoy a beer and a Cornish pasty at the match later, but the breakfast was fantastic, and we couldn't resist overeating except for the beans. Although they were fine, I personally still couldn't get used to beans for breakfast. This is an experience that we learned from for the future matches we attended. England gets a bad rap for their food, but I enjoyed what they had to offer, except perhaps for the blood sausage, which I did not care for much, texture or taste wise. We walked from the hotel to Fratton Park, a 21,000-capacity stadium. Some of the English residential architecture and style took a second to get used to as the front door was right up to the sidewalk where the public would stroll by, but it was charming, especially with neighbors in such close proximity. The town appeared to be tight knit. Passing a local who seemed to be in a rush carrying his groceries home, he asked us what time kick off was. This interaction felt like we were part of the community. Once we made it to the stadium, we were sort of lost as to where to enter. We ran into one of the stewards, Abdul, who we found out later was sort of a local legend at Fratton Park. He pointed us in the right direction. We actually had to walk through this tiny sliver of space between two walls to get to our entrance. It was a bit strange having to do that and reminiscent of the *Harry Potter* novels, as many things in England seemed to be. On our way up, the inside walls of the stadium were plastered with former Pompey players, including former Croatian international Robert Prosinečki as he played one season there and left an indelible mark on the Pompey faithful. Of course, I had to get a selfie standing next to the picture of my Balkan brother. Getting to our seats and getting a view of the whole stadium helped us truly appreciate Fratton Park, referred to as the Old Girl, even more than walking up to the iconic mock Tudor entrance. Its age and size only added to its charm. As to the match, Pompey was in contention to move up to the Championship and this was an important match to continue that quest. To our right was a group of middle-aged men, who, by demeanor and tattoos, surely appeared to have enjoyed a proper scrap when they were younger. To our left, a father with two small boys, indoctrinating them into the beautiful game. Roaring chants of "Play Up Pompey" to the tune of the Westminster Chimes filled the stadium along with "Blue Army" (which we were not familiar with and we foolishly followed the little boy's lead who was saying "Who Are They?!") It was a raucous atmosphere. Pompey went down in the 9th minute but equalized in the 66th minute through a Tom Naylor header from a corner. The atmosphere in the stadium was expectant, and the energy of the lads on the pitch clearly telegraphed that there was more to come. I elbowed my wife 16 minutes later and shouted, "start filming, they're gonna score!" It was an accurate prediction; Pompey went up 2-1 through Brett Pittman from a half-volley inside the box. Pompey saw the match out and the supporters went home happy. After the match, we walked from Fortress Fratton to the historic dockyard to tour the HMS Victory. Along the way, we were hailed by a bloke asking, "did we win?" to which my beaming wife replied "yes, *we* did." After a long day, we finally went back to our room to sleep, only to be awoken after midnight to an inebriated fellow walking down the street singing "Play Up Pompey." This town was in love with its club and identified with it through and through.

 We arrived in London a few days later after taking the train from Portsmouth. Besides enjoying the English countryside and the sights of London, including the changing of the guard at Buckingham Palace, where I seemed to hear different languages at every turn of the head spoken by other tourists, and eating bangers & mash, we would catch the derby between Manchester United and Manchester City at a pub near our hotel. The English are known for their involved presence and atmospheres at the pub during football matches, so we wanted to check off another item from our bucket list. The match was significant for City as they were in a title race with Liverpool. Would United be able to stop City from gaining that advantage? Turns out they would not. A Bernardo Silva goal in the 54th minute and a Leroy Sané goal in the 66th minute would be enough to beat the Red Devils and put them ahead of Liverpool by one point with three matches remaining in the season. Although we were in London, the pub patrons' eyes were fixed on the match. Each missed chance would draw an "ooh" or "ahh" from them. When City scored their first goal, the pub exploded in jubilation. Who knows if these people were supporters of either team or wanted City to falter because they were Liverpool fans. They may have been just enjoying the spectacle as football fans or got caught up in the mindset of the crowd. Whatever the reason, this proper pub atmosphere certainly made the match more interesting and exciting than without it.

The next day we paid a visit to Chelsea's Stamford Bridge for a stadium tour. I was determined to at least go to one football ground while we were in one of the great cities of the world. We chose Stamford Bridge due to my wife's long-held soft-spot for Chelsea. She got her very first football merch after winning a fitness competition on her middle school soccer team. The blue and white Chelsea scarf matched her school jersey, and quickly joined the United States National Team pennant in a place of honor hanging above her dresser in her childhood bedroom. However, I appreciated Stamford Bridge more for its ease of access and distance from our hotel. We took the famous London Underground ("The Tube") and got off at Fulham Broadway station. The stadium was a very short walk from the tube station and the surrounding neighborhood was extremely posh. Outside of the stadium was a statue of Peter Osgood, who I learned was a Chelsea legend from the 1960s/70s. He won an FA Cup and a European Cup Winners' Cup with the team in 1970 and 1971, respectively. Upon entering the facility, we were gathered with the rest of our tour group who were no more than ten people. Headsets were provided that allowed the tour to be listened to in other languages for those that did not speak English. Our tour guide was a chap by the name of Nigel, an older gentleman who had been a Chelsea supporter since he was a little boy. His enthusiasm for the club during the entirety of the tour, even in his older age, seemed genuine and authentic and made us appreciate the tour more than we would have. Chelsea's museum was a treat for me as a football history buff. It included banners, pictures of legends, and replica trophies that the club had won throughout the years, including the Champions League trophy, which I always dreamed of taking a picture with. After visiting the locker rooms, we walked through the tunnel and sat pitch side while Nigel continued to give us tidbits about the club. Sitting there from that viewpoint, the stadium looks massive with its 40,000+ capacity. It seems to come down on you like a huge tidal wave on the ocean. We moved up to a different part of the stadium and Nigel pointed out to us that just a section or two over is where the players' wives and girlfriends (WAGs) would sit during matches. One of our fellow tourists, immediately asked "What about John Terry?" It seemed that no one got the joke besides myself, my wife, and Nigel, who took it gracefully on the chin and responded in kind. The joke being that John Terry would have difficulty bringing both his wife and mistress after rumors came about of him having one. One of the last bits before the tour concluded was to visit the press room where you could take pictures sitting at the table where the manager would speak to the press after matches. Of course, I had to indulge and snap a photo of myself sitting where legendary managers such as Claudio Ranieri and José Mourinho had sat. After that, the tour concluded. Although I am not a Chelsea fan or sympathizer, the tour itself was well worth it, if only for the history behind the club and to tour a famous stadium.

Up next was our trip to Germany for the Ruhr Derby between Dortmund and Schalke. More than anything, the trip was for nostalgia. We took the "Chunnel" train from London, under the English Channel, into France with a stop in the Netherlands. The train from there would take us to Köln and then to Mülheim an der Ruhr. We arrived in the center of town where a shopping center called Forum was attached to the train and bus stations. The old familiar sight was a tall circular building with its name on top in red. We were staying with family friends. They awaited us at the station and helped us with our luggage. We walked through the station's various paths and walkways and my foggy memories became concrete reality once again. They lived near the train station; a small mercy, since it was nearing midnight, and we were exhausted from traveling all day. Upon arrival, a smorgasbord of Bosnian food had been prepared for us. It was a kingly feast that we were not expecting. When we were nodding off at the table, stuffed to the gills with more dishes than I could put a name to, we were finally allowed to retire for the night. We woke up the next morning to an equally majestic spread for breakfast. We were truly treated to Bosnian hospitality. After breakfast, it was time to walk the streets and see the sights that I once called my home. As a kid, everything looks bigger to you. Walking the main strip in Mülheim as an adult now, everything seemed smaller. All the buildings remained intact; however, the McDonald's that I would visit as a kid was not there anymore and some of the department stores were gone too. Instead of taking the tram and bus that I would have taken as a kid to go to school, our map app indicated it was only a thirty-minute walk from where we were staying, which surprised me. The adrenaline was rushing through me; I was excited to see my elementary school again. We crossed the Schlossbrücke (Castle Bridge), underneath which the Ruhr River runs. Spring snow thaw had quickened the flow of the normally gentle river. My wife and I stopped for a moment to watch leaves floating tranquilly under the bridge before getting caught up in the swirling eddies on the backside of the rounded stone piers. We passed the castle Broich on the other side and continued passing through residential areas and walked up a great hill. And there it was, in all its brick-and-mortar glory, my elementary school. We walked around and snapped a few photos. The little store outside of the elementary school still existed, just as I remembered. As a kid, I would stop there before school to buy Panini stickers for the 1998 World Cup and Bundesliga seasons, and I would enthusiastically trade them with my classmates. I was beaming; the memories just overcame me. We did not visit the site where the refugee camp was located, as that already had been torn down while we were still living in Germany. After I got my fill of school nostalgia, we turned around and stopped at a pub down the street from the school for a quick beer. It was served in a tiny glass that my wife joked must be the size meant for the elementary students. Little did I know that we walked into a Schalke supporters' pub – luckily, we did not have any Dortmund clothing on at that moment! We returned to our hosts and were picked up by a childhood friend of mine, Ado, who I had not seen in nearly twenty years. We would stay with them for the duration of our stay in Germany.

They lived in a town nearby, not too far from Mülheim. Ado and his family also managed to stay in Germany permanently post-war. It was wonderful to embrace my dear friend and his hard-working family again. We reminisced about the old times and what had been going on with our lives up until now, while at the mercy of Bosnian hospitality once again. We ended up walking to a nearby Doner Kebab shop for some substantial food after hours of reminiscing over while being politely strong-armed into countless rounds of cheese, cured meats, cookies, cakes, coffee, candy, and other small snacks. A doner kebab is like a gyro introduced to the Germans by Turkish guest workers in Berlin in the early 1970s. It is one of the top-selling street foods in Germany that I had many times when I lived there and it was nice to bite into one of these delicatessen once again. Once the food coma came about, it was time to hit the hay in anticipation of the big football day.

The next day was the Ruhr Derby. Saturday, April 27, 2019. I could not sleep the night before. This was perhaps the main reason I came to Germany. I had packed my 1997 Borussia Dortmund home jersey to wear to the match. I bought this shirt online only a couple of years before as one of my first steps in the quest to lay my nostalgia to rest. This jersey helped fill a void that had been in my soul. As I said, I did not have a Dortmund jersey as a kid as it was hard to come by where we lived. Some small part of me was always bothered by that lack, even years after we left Germany and football faded from my life. Now I was an adult with the means to make my inner child's dreams come true. Kick off was 15:30 local time so we left around noon. Ado's younger brother, Mo, who was still a baby back in 1999, drove us to the train station. Complementary train tickets were part of the match day ticket, so we hopped on the train to Dortmund. Each stop picked up more and more Dortmund fans. Soon, our train car acquired a fella who was selling beer in Dortmund themed cups with star players on them. More accurately, and this is key for legal reasons, *with the purchase of a cup* came a complementary beer. My German was very rusty so we nervously spoke up in English with the intent of trying to buy a beer or two, hoping he would understand us. He did, and we ended up speaking to him briefly about our travels and the upcoming match. It was nice to mingle with local BVB fans and get a glimpse of that local support.

We arrived in downtown Dortmund at the Dortmund Hauptbahnhof (Dortmund main railway station). We weren't exactly sure which direction to take to the stadium, so we asked security and they basically pointed and told us to follow the other people dressed in black and yellow. We did but it turned out that the group of Dortmund fans we were following went to a pub instead of the stadium. We used our map app to get us where we needed to go. We finally ended up on a street with hundreds and hundreds of Dortmund fans flowing like a river. Little stands were open selling food and beer. We tried a beer called Kronen for the first time, a beer that had been around since the Middle Ages, as we continued our march to the stadium. One supporter in front of us had stolen a Schalke scarf and allowed other supporters to stomp or kick this trophy of war. The march to the stadium reminded me of what you see in those Ultra videos where there is a unified group of people marching in formation like they are about to go to war.

One could not fully see the stadium in the direction we were coming from. Streets, buildings, and trees obstructed the view. However, once we got past that, there it was in all its glory, the Westfalenstadion ("Signal Iduna Park" for sponsorship reasons), one of football's loudest stadiums that is filled to the brim every home game. With its 81,365 capacity, it cracks as one of the biggest stadiums in Europe and average attendance is always near the top of the football charts. Since it was a derby, security was extra heavy. Before finding our seats, we needed to immerse ourselves in the full German football experience with classic stadium fare and good German beer. Dortmund's payment system for those types of goods was cash-less. You had to get a card in the stadium and load money onto it and use the card to buy items you desired. We stood in a quickly moving queue, and I could hardly make up my mind on which of the delicious options to choose from before it was our turn to order. I decided on the bratwurst, and my wife bought a pretzel. Oh how I had missed the *brötchen*! This German bread roll that would be eaten with the sausage was perfection. The *brötchen* just hit completely different than any of the bread back in the States. The first bite made me recall all those times my mother would make my lunch in elementary school with this specific bread and the various sandwich meats and cheeses she would put on it. The flavor triggered my memory for those minutes that we stood there underneath the stands eating. We downed our food with Brinkhoff's, another local Dortmund beer which was advertised all over the stadium. It was a perfect pairing for food at a football match.

It was time to walk up the steps into a German stadium, just like I had done decades before. Reaching the top and then shuffling down the row to our seats in the eastern part of the stadium, I saw the black and yellow painted sections all over the stadium. Dortmund's ultras that camp out in the Südtribüne (South stand – the free-standing section in the stadium) were slowly beginning to create the atmosphere that has made them world famous. The Yellow Wall was being built brick by brick as I watched. I took it all in. I was overwhelmingly happy and grateful to be here now, after I did not make it when I was a kid.

Close to us were the Schalke fans, who also brought an atmosphere and a wall of noise of their own. The tension, no, *hatred* in the air between the two clubs and their supporters was palpable. Our section and the Schalke section were divided by black nets from floor to ceiling so that people would not be hit if a projectile was hurled our way and vice versa. What added to the atmosphere were the high stakes involved in this match. Dortmund was in a very tight title race with FC Bayern München. Bayern had won the league the previous six years and were working towards their seventh consecutive title, while the last time Dortmund had won the league was in the 2011-2012 season. A seventh consecutive title for Bayern would not look good for the league. Moreover, this was the first true title race in many years as Bayern's previous six titles were won comfortably by a wide margin in the table. Neutrals (and Dortmund fans) wanted a title race, and they wanted a different winner. Anyone but Bayern! Going into this matchday, Bayern led by one point. Dortmund needed to win to keep up the pressure and, with four matchdays left to play, there was not room for any error. For Schalke, while they were fourth from the bottom and flirting with relegation, nothing else would be sweeter than sticking a dagger into the title hopes of their eternal enemy.

We were getting closer to kick off and several Dortmund staples were hitting the stadium speakers in addition to the songs and chants the Yellow Wall was belting out. Song wise, I was looking forward to "You'll Never Walk Alone" a staple adopted by Dortmund and inspired by Glasgow Celtic in the early 90s. Liverpool's rendition is of course the most famous one. It is a slow, sweet, sentimental piece that we danced to at our wedding, so standing there next to each other, slowly swaying back and forth while holding Dortmund scarves above our heads and singing the song, was a lovely reminder of the promises we made to each other a few weeks back. It added a personal touch to the momentous occasion that we were experiencing.

Dortmund got off to a red-hot start. Mario Götze, who started at the club as a youth and spent four seasons with the senior side before controversially moving to Bayern in 2013 and then returning to BVB in 2016, headed home a flick into the top right corner from English starlet Jadon Sancho's assist and BVB was up 1-0. A fast start for Dortmund and delirium hit the BVB supporters in the stadium. Chants of "Wer Wird Deutscher Meister?! BVB Borussia!" (Who will be German champions?! BVB Borussia) began after the goal. The lead would be short lived as the referee adjudged a handball in the box by Julian Weigl and Schalke player Daniel Caligiuri sent Roman Bürki the wrong way while calmly placing it in the bottom, right-hand corner. Only ten minutes later, Schalke's Salif Sané scored with a header from a set-piece and Schalke was up 2-1. Small inklings of doubt began to creep into the heads of the Dortmund faithful. Dortmund is not known for keeping a mentally sharp and tough consistency, so it was not necessarily a surprise that this was happening. However, when the title race is on the line, supporters expect more. They expect more focus and concentration. However, there was hope. After all, this was a derby and crazier things have happened before. Going into half time, the match remained 2-1.

We grabbed another Brinkhoff's and made a pit-stop in the bathroom before the second half kicked off. Disaster struck in the 60th minute as BVB legend, Marco Reus, tackled a Schalke player from behind, leading to a straight red. The resulting free kick by Caligiuri put Schalke up 3-1. Down a player and 2 goals behind, a comeback seemed insurmountable. The Schalke fans began mocking the Dortmund fans by sarcastically singing "Wer wird Deutscher Meister?! BVB Borussia." Absolute silence and despondency hit the BVB supporters' spirits. Could it get any worse at this point when you're down a man and down two goals in a derby? Not to mention when you are in the closest title race in years? The answer is yes. It could get worse. After Reus was sent off, only five minutes later, Marius Wolf was sent off for almost an identical foul. A straight red card reduced Dortmund to nine players. However, Dortmund pushed on, scoring after Witsel practically tapped the ball in from a headed cross in the 84th minute. It was a lifeline, albeit a small one, for two minutes. Schalke struck only two minutes later via Breel Embolo and that was all she wrote. A dagger into the hearts of the BVB players and their fans. The Schalke fans were delirious as it was another three points in pursuit of avoiding relegation and because they played spoiler to Dortmund's title hopes. Beers were thrown in our direction and a lot of middle fingers. We made our way down the steps, shoulders slouched, in silence. We walked back to the train station disappointed, disillusioned, and pissed off at what we had just experienced. Later, I found out that several of the Dortmund ultras attempted to go into the

Schalke section to confront and fight Schalke fans. Tempers clearly boiled over because of what was at stake.

Once we made it back to Oberhausen, we were picked up by Ado's little brother, Mo, and we all went back to their house. A few hours later, Denis, another friend from my childhood at The Container, made an appearance. Word got around that I was visiting Germany, so he made it a priority to come see me. He used to be one of the shorter guys in our childhood group and now he was much taller than me. Besides playing football with him, I used to play video games with him all the time. Back in the day, Denis had two gaming consoles, the Super Nintendo and the PlayStation 1. We would spend hours and hours playing the Street Fighter games and FIFA 98: Road to the World Cup. Because of his personal situation, he was able to permanently stay in Germany as well. We, too, reminisced and spoke about what was currently going on with our lives. It was a joy to see two friends from our "Mali Šarafi" group.

Nostalgia is a funny thing. I saw childhood friends and their families again. I saw my elementary school again. I saw the Ruhr River and walked through the center of the city and ate local cuisine and I was able to show it all to my new bride. Regardless of the result, I also fulfilled my childhood dream of seeing Dortmund at the Westfalenstadion. Before this trip, I always had some small desire to return to Germany permanently.

Despite my status as a refugee, my childhood was pretty pleasant. I liked the efficient way the Germans ran their country and certain aspects of their culture. I also longed for the good old days, the carefree environment, the different architecture, and the common familiarity amongst the folk. However, after this trip, I realized two things. The thing that I longed for did not exist anymore. The world seems much rosier when seen through a child's eyes, after all. The world had changed. People moved and people changed. Part of me was living in the past. The second thing I realized was that this nostalgia existed because I did not leave properly. I felt like I left a part of me behind in Germany, like my original stay in Germany had not been completed and in the dark recesses in the back of my mind I was waiting to somehow be sucked back into that life I had been so suddenly ripped out of. Now that I had seen these beloved people from my childhood once again and said a proper goodbye to them, now that I had walked the city's streets in full awareness of my impending departure, and with knowledge of what awaited me in the United States, it finally felt complete. The desire to return permanently was extinguished within me.

Ado dropped us off at the train station the next morning to continue our journey. Our next stop would be Vienna, Austria to see my two cousins and their mother. Our train took us to Nurnberg and then from there to Vienna. Traveling through the mountains in Bavaria and Austria was exceptionally picturesque. The snowy mountains were pushing up against us – it reminded me of the film *Murder on the Orient Express* – with its dramatic scenery that would change in a flash as we went through tunnels or tight, forested passes that suddenly opened up into stunning views of a wide valley, the patchwork farmland stretching from one rocky slope to the other and quaint alpine houses on the edge of a crystal clear mountain lake. The train took more time than a short hop flight, but it was definitely worth the investment. We were greeted at the station by my cousin, who I had not seen in nearly twenty years. She took us to her mother's house, and we saw her and my other cousin (her sister). We stayed in Vienna for a few days and enjoyed what the city had to offer in terms of its beautiful, traditional architecture including the majestic Schönbrunn Palace, its coffee houses, restaurants, and historical buildings and of course the mini-family reunion.

We continued our journey to Zagreb, Croatia via train with our ultimate destination being Dubrovnik on the Adriatic coast. On our way from Vienna to Zagreb, the train attendant came by to check tickets as is normal. I, not understanding or speaking Austrian German, did not catch the meaning when he said something additional. He repeated it in heavily accented, broken English but I still couldn't understand what he was trying to convey. Eventually, some helpful passenger sitting across the aisle interpreted for us a bit better. Basically, the train attendant was telling us we would have to get off at a certain stop because the direct route was blocked by construction on the train tracks. I have never experienced such a cold sweat before in my life nor in such a quick fashion. No one told us about this change before we got on the train. For me, there is nothing worse than having plans change without timely notice, especially in a foreign country where I am not familiar with the surroundings and workings of public transport. While I am processing this information and wondering what in blue blazes we are going to do (and my wife is watching me sweat cold bullets and is nearly cracking a rib laughing at me), the attendant walked by once again and through our fellow passenger told us that a bus would pick us up at the stop, take us to a town in Slovenia, and then we would catch a train there to Zagreb. What a relief! At least half of my undershirt had been soaked with sweat. My wife required ten minutes and a Kleenex to get her laughing fit under control.

    We arrived in Zagreb only an hour later than expected. After getting out of the train station, we wandered onto the dark street. Streetlights reflected off the puddles on the asphalt. The area around the station was completely deserted as it was around 22:30. We eventually managed to take a rideshare to my aunt's flat (technically one of my far-removed cousins but she's elderly so I call her my aunt). I had not seen her since 1992. My family stayed with her back then while we were waiting on immigration bureaucracy to go to Germany. Again, another great meal awaited us at 23:00. There was not much time to chat since we were exhausted and because we had to get up in the early morning hours to catch our flight to Dubrovnik. Five hours later we were awake and caught a taxi to Zagreb airport for our flight to the city on the coast. The flight lasted a little over an hour – we landed at a tiny airport where we disembarked directly onto the tarmac. It was a very leisurely ride to the hotel, and we enjoyed 180° views of the scenic coastline to one side while winding along the steep slopes of arid rockface that somehow managed to support wildflowers and small olive trees. We arrived several hours before check-in time and left our luggage at the front desk. This allowed us to kill some time and walk around to explore the city.

We walked through the steep streets of Dubrovnik and enjoyed seeing the marina and all the yachts and sail boats gently bobbing on the azure water. The hills with homes built into their sides were a sight to behold; the emphasis on vertical building meant that many houses on the uphill side of the street would have a basement garage and the houses on the other side had their cars parked on the roof, level with the road. I had never been to a coastal city like this – even in Portsmouth the architecture and buildings were quite different. More than that, the people made their personal mark on the city through street art, and nowhere did we see the sterile landscapes and cookie-cutter houses of American suburbia. There was very little grass or ornamental invasive plants, instead, each small plot had beautiful citrus trees or lovingly supported olive trees with netting strung beneath to catch the fruit. Many homes boasted artwork in the form of pottery or ornate garden walls. We came across a beautiful mural on a wall that paid tribute to Hajduk Split, the "local" team so to speak. Split was nearly three hours northwest along the Adriatic Coast, but the people in Dubrovnik were not only fellow coastal people with their counterparts in Split, but they were also from the same region – Dalmatia. Their biggest rival was Dinamo from the capital, Zagreb. This is called the "Eternal Derby." The head-to-head pre-Yugoslavia break-up was almost 50/50, but post-break up, Dinamo had accumulated the better overall record. As for me, I was pleased football sights and history were back on the menu after not seeing anything football related in Vienna.

On our trek back to the hotel, we came across some trees with fruits that my amateur horticulturist of a wife was not familiar with except that it was some sort of citrus. My adventurous wife decided to pluck one but saved it until we returned to the hotel. As we returned to the hotel, we still had a little bit of time before check-in, so we sat in the lobby. My wife decided she was going to try this fruit now. The hotel clerk keenly watched her and knew something that we did not. She bit into the fruit that turned out to be bitter and not edible. The clerk walked over with a garbage can, smirking to himself, so that my wife could spit out this disgusting comestible. I could not help but laugh. This was my revenge from the cold sweat train ride from Vienna.

After some rest and relaxation, we decided to walk around as more places were open now and we were in search of drinks and dinner. We found a very inviting spot a short walk from the hotel. Because Dubrovnik is a tourist spot, many individuals in the service industry speak English quite well. And since English was my best language, spoken and written, I figured I would play it safe and stick to it since I did not want to run the risk of not understanding something in Croatian or local dialect and looking like an idiot. We ordered our meal. I tried fried octopus for the first time, as well as deep-fried whole sardines. At some point early in the dinner, I decided to drop the "only English language" act and spoke with the owner, David, and the waiter freely in Serbo-Croatian. I needed a little bit more comfort and confidence I suppose. After I told him where we lived in the States, he told us he had been there during the civil war in the

1990s and described certain sights from Mobile. I was taken aback and surprised. The world is indeed a small place. David is a Hajduk Split fan but supported Liverpool in England. This was good timing as Liverpool faced Barcelona in the first leg of the semifinals of the Champions League. He invited us back the following evening for the match. The next day we got up early to experience all Dubrovnik had to offer. Our first destination was Dubrovnik's "Old Town." On the bus to Old Town, I was wearing my AFC Mobile jersey. An older American lady asked me whether I was from Mobile, Alabama. Questions like these by strangers tend to make me think about my personal identity and with whom or what I identify. I gave her a short summary about my background while holding on to the bar on the bus. She and her travel companion were from Pennsylvania. It was a pleasant conversation, but also a reminder of the life-long question of "who am I?" and that the trip was only a few days from being over.

Dubrovnik's "Old Town" was a medieval city that also acted as a fortress during those ancient times. Standing atop the walkable walls, one could see the beautiful, crystal-clear Adriatic Sea. There were centuries of history in these walls, and you are transported to a different, simpler time when you are behind the Old Town's Pile Gate. Within the town are also restaurants and shops. The city had been well preserved over the centuries and even made its name to a worldwide audience when part of *Game of Thrones* was filmed there, namely the scenes highlighting the architecture of King's Landing. The port of the city was also active. We took a ferry to an island named Lokrum which offered a Benedictine monastery, a botanical garden, another *Game of Thrones* filming location where one could take a picture sitting on the actual Iron Throne, and other historical scenery. Peacocks strutted all across the island and the pathways were flanked by lush vegetation. While touring the monastery, we came across a man wearing a Sheffield United kit, prompting my wife to quickly quip "Up the Blades!" He returned the response in kind only for his own wife to laugh at the exchange. After a long, hot, and enjoyable day exploring Lokrum and the Old Town, we were ready to head back to the modern city. We had one more stop to make before we returned to the hotel. Leaving through the Pile Gate, a moment of tourist idiocy came upon us. We knew we needed to take a bus to the shopping center by the harbor that we walked past on the day of our arrival. We spotted the bus that would be taking that route and began making our way to the bus stop, but the bus began to pull away from the curb! We started running after it. We were the only people running… and we missed it. We weren't aware of how frequently the busses would come and were cursing to high heaven about missing it as we walked with hung heads and drooping shoulders back to the bus stop…only to find out that the next bus was coming within five minutes. We felt like idiots.

I wanted to get to the shopping center before it closed for the evening. My mission was to purchase a tracksuit, playing to the stereotype of a Slav in his traditional clothing. Although I had several at home, it only felt right for me to purchase one in the depth of the former Yugoslavia in the dragon lair. The pot of gold was found along with some black trainers. My Slavic armor had been complete. I was Yugo Man!

After dropping off our purchases in our hotel room, we made our way back to the same spot for dinner from the previous evening and for camaraderie as we watched the match. I greatly enjoyed the opportunity to chat about football in my first language with David. Those opportunities did not present themselves much back in Alabama, only with my dad and his friend Siniša. The sense of cultural familiarity was an echo of what I experienced on my trip to St. Louis several years prior. We switched fluidly between Serbo-Croatian and English, using whichever words came to mind quicker. A group of English women sat next to our table and overheard the English-language portion of our conversation and pitched in with their excitement that Norwich City would be returning to the Premier League the following season. We bid farewell to David and thanked him for his hospitality. The next day, we returned to Zagreb to spend the day with my aunt, her sister (my other aunt), and a cousin, enjoying the limited time that we had left on our trip. The center of Zagreb, while historic and beautiful, had a bit too much graffiti for my liking. Early next morning, we departed from Zagreb to Frankfurt. Our flight arrived a little late and we were in the security line for our flight to the US. The clock was ticking, and we were worried that we would miss our flight. After we got through security, we ran to our gate. It was my "run through the airport and make it cinematic-looking" moment. We made it just in time. The plane waited for us and we were the last people to board. I was drenched in sweat and the flight attendant offered me a cup of water. Crisis averted. We buckled up and we were airborne.

Upon reflection, it was great to see the old continent again. New faces and old, familiar sights and novel experiences, the exhaustion of travel and the reinvigoration of having been snapped out of the daily grind, I felt that a door had been closed and another opened. The nostalgia void had finally been filled inside me and I became unstuck from the past. Time had moved on in Europe and I too was ready to move forward.

CHAPTER 12

Reignited Passion

Somewhere I Belong

Around the time of planning the wedding, the monotony of watching European football was creeping in. Each league and its teams used to have a particular style of play, but over the last decade that changed. I suspect there were several reasons: more movement by players and coaches and the easy availability of information (from coaching strategies and philosophies, tactics, training and minute statistical details about matches and players, etc.). Generally, individuality and creativity were constricted in play and frowned upon with few exceptions. The trend tended to be towards more and more standardization. The top teams in the top leagues played a similar type of football to me. It wasn't as magical as it was before. So, I needed something new. I figured the next best place to search for authentic football would be in South America. I remembered that my father used to watch the Argentinian league in the late 2000s and my short sojourn with Juliano during graduate school planted the seed for a cataclysmic event in my football life. I remembered the name Boca Juniors and as luck would have it, I came across a documentary on the team. It mesmerized me. The passion, the authenticity, the working-class background, the legendary and creative players like Juan Román Riquelme, Diego Maradona, and Martín Palermo who donned the blue and gold colors altogether won me over and had me hooked. I felt like a kid again with the discovery of something "new" even though this was all in history. As coincidence would have it, Boca would play their archrival, their eternal enemy, River Plate in the Copa Libertadores final in November 2018. This was to determine the champion of South America's premier continental competition. As a new fan, the first Boca match I would watch was the first leg of the tie at La Bombonera on November 10, 2018. However, the natural elements had other ideas. It rained so heavily in Buenos Aires on that day, that the pitch at the Bombonera was waterlogged. The match was rescheduled to take place a day later. There was also the issue of where I was going to watch this match. A few local Mexican restaurants typically showed matches from Central and South American countries, so I called one and they indeed planned on showing it. This coincided with lunch time so I took my fiancée and my parents to the restaurant. This was also a popular spot for the local bourgeoisie. So here I am, a

Bosnian-American in a Mexican restaurant surrounded by mostly Americans, having my eyes glued to the screen to watch two Argentinian teams battle it out for South American football supremacy. When Ramón "Wanchope" Ábila scored and subsequently Darío "Pipa" Benedetto before the first half finished, I let out exuberant celebrations that got me certain looks from the non-football believers. Ultimately, the match finished 2-2 and the winner would have to be decided at River Plate's El Monumental on November 24, 2018. However, the second leg would not take place that day. River Plate fans attacked the bus that carried Boca players. The windows on the bus were shattered which allowed pepper spray to also enter the bus. Boca did not want to play under these conditions; they wanted to play in equal conditions as River did in the first leg. Numerous cities offered their hospitality to host the second leg. Because of safety concerns by CONMEBOL, the match would ultimately take place in Madrid, Spain. The irony was not lost. A South American competition called the "Copa Libertadores," named after the liberators and in honor of the leaders who fought for independence from Spain would take place in Spain.

I repeated what I did for the second leg. Although Boca scored first, River equalized in the 68th minute and due to the teams being tied on aggregate, the match went into extra time. River scored again in the 109th minute and Boca attacked wave after wave and even hitting the post, but the football gods would not be on their side. River countered when Boca was throwing every player into attack and scored. River won 3-1 and 5-3 on aggregate. My new club that I fell for lost, but suffering together made me love them even more.

The following year, I followed the club's Libertadores campaign again, where they came up short in the semi-finals against River Plate *again*, losing 2-1 on aggregate. It was not until March 7, 2020 when I would "get it." It being my full indoctrination into Boca fandom. The COVID-19 pandemic and shutdown had just begun, and it did not fully reach Argentina yet. Boca's final match of the campaign would be against Gimnasia, managed by Maradona. Maradona would receive an icon's welcome even though he coached the other team. He was a Boca legend, having played for them in 1981 and winning the Metropolitano. He then returned towards the tail-end of his career in 1995. He played his last professional match with the club on October 25, 1997. Conspicuously missing from the welcome was Juan Román Riquelme, who had been recently elected as second vice president on a ticket with Jorge Amor Ameal and Mario Pergolini. Maradona and Riquelme had a huge falling out before the World Cup in 2010 and were not on speaking terms with one another. After the festivities for Maradona concluded, Riquelme made it to the stadium and sat in his VP Box, drinking his yerba mate and maintaining his poker face.

For Boca to win the league, they would have to win their match and River would have to drop points in theirs. In River's match against Atlético Tucumán, the latter would take the lead until Matías Suárez equalized for River in the 35th minute. As things stood, River would be champions. However, another Boca legend, Carlos Tevez, who had just returned from his unsuccessful stint in China, had other ideas. He would be the one to break the deadlock in the 72nd minute with a thunderous strike that the Gimnasia keeper could not parry away. Tevez climbed the fence in celebration and an iconic picture was born of it. The last twenty minutes remained tense. I was pacing back and forth in the living room. Numerous fans at the stadium had radios and word was coming in that the River match finished in a draw. The whistle blew in La Bombonera and the words quickly filtered to the players. The celebrations erupted. Tevez was hoisted on other's shoulders. Riquelme was holding his mate and his thermos with a slight smile appearing on his face. This was my first time watching Boca winning and celebrating a title. Seeing the fans in the stands reach new levels of exuberance, plus their non-stop singing during the match, made me realize that this was the passion that I was longing for. These fans breathed the club in their daily lives. This is what I wanted and needed. The research about the club and the neighborhood it was based out of continued over the next month. I fell in football love all over again.

As a result of this newfound passion, in June 2020, while the COVID pandemic was still at its height, I became an international socio of the club. I had never been a card-carrying member of any football club, but this just felt right. When you're at home, you know you're at home. My fanaticism continued when we bought our first house shortly afterwards. I now had the freedom to make another small dream come true: creating a football room with. Before we even started to move in, I would paint it in blue and yellow. We spent the next several months carefully mounting, hanging, and arranging all the various pictures, plaques, and other miscellaneous items of the beautiful game that we had acquired over the years and had been unable to properly display in our tiny apartment. My wife's grandfather helped greatly in turning my vision into reality – he is a skilled artist and handyman. He gifted us hand painted wooden crests of: Argentina, Boca Juniors, AFC Mobile, Portsmouth, Dortmund, and Napoli (for whom I have a soft spot for). He built and installed a trophy shelf over the TV, where some of the items would be displayed. The shrine that I called my sanctuary had been completed in a place I now called my home.

Detour - About Diego – D10S Is Dead

Of course, I was not old enough to watch "El Diego" in his prime nor did I have a chance to watch him at the end of his career. Again, it was through tales from my father, video clips on YouTube, articles on the internet, and speaking with others that I heard of and learned about demi-god Diego Armando Maradona. It was not until the documentary about him directed by Asif Kapadia that I finally understood why Maradona was proclaimed the greatest of all time. It was the moment it clicked for me. He dragged Argentina to World Cup victory in 1986 and helped win Napoli not one but two league titles which were the only two in their history until the 2022/2023 season. With Napoli, he also won a Coppa Italia and the UEFA Cup. He reached another World Cup final with Argentina in an injured state and lost due to a controversial penalty to the Germans. His last trophy with Argentina would be the Artemio Franchi Cup, a Supercup of sorts between the current Copa America and European Cup winners, in 1993. Countless personal accolades followed him. He was charismatic and his personality infectious. It is difficult to describe in words the effect, intangible and tangible, that he's had on the footballing world, people, and his country of Argentina. I have tried my best to pay tribute to him in this book and it was in November 2020 that he personally affected my life for the first time, outside of buying his jerseys and watching YouTube clips of him.

I woke up late on the morning of November 25, 2020. It was the day before Thanksgiving in the States. I didn't have to work that day, so I woke up later than usual, made myself breakfast, and began browsing the internet. I started reading social media posts that Maradona had died. Surely, it could not be the truth. There had been rumors in the past that Maradona had died but they turned out to be nasty hoaxes – unfortunately this one was not one of those. Once the big channels and websites began to discuss it, it was confirmed. The shock that came over me. His death caused a big hole in the world of football. For me personally, it was like a distant family member had died. I called my father and told him in a wavering voice, "The greatest footballer of all time just died." I was glued to the computer for a while, just reading, hoping that everyone was wrong and that it was another cruel prank played on the footballing world. However, nothing changed. In the afternoon, Keath Kaufmann from the local soccer group planned an impromptu gathering at a local bar. On the way over, I stopped to get gas, wearing my Diego jersey from the 1986 World Cup. A Hispanic gentleman was also pumping his gas and noticed my jersey and we briefly exchanged comments mourning Diego's death. The TVs at the bar were showing news about his passing. Many of us would take a shot of tequila and chant "Olé, olé, olé, olé, Diego, Diego!" Here I was with my American friends who liked the sport honoring and paying tribute to Diego Maradona. It is not something I ever imagined. It was surreal. I never expected this type of response. I thought I was just going to sit at home, have a drink in his honor, and continue to watch the tributes pour in. His death brought our small group together again after COVID had canceled AFC Mobile's 2020 season. The football world grieved, and the football world paid him tribute, not only on that day, but even weeks later. One picture that stuck with me was of a Boca fan and a River fan hugging each other in tears, fans of two eternal rivals that divide Argentina heavily, mourning Diego's death. The power of Maradona's death was visible. With his death, the legend and myth grew. I became an even bigger fan of his. Although Maradona wrestled with his personal demons and some of his behavior had been very questionable, the thing that matters, as the saying goes, is "not what he did with his life, but what he did for ours."

Back on Track

After becoming a member of Boca Juniors in June 2020, I wanted to see them live and in person. However, it would be another two years before that would happen and my best man, Juliano, would be the impetus. He popped the question to his significant other, and we were invited to the wedding. Since he made the trip for mine, I had to return the favor. It was time to visit the land of Ronaldo, Pelé, and Zico. We took a long journey to Brasília, the capital. On the way to Brasília on our last flight, the passenger sitting next to me had a medical emergency. I woke up to someone aggressively fanning him and was confused in my grogginess. They hustled us to a different part of the plane, half-awake and leaving all of our possessions behind, so the guy could lay down across our entire row of seats. We had no idea what happened to the guy to cause him to go into medical distress. Luckily, he came out alright, and the flight just continued. We landed in Brasília a little after dawn where the groom and bride-to-be picked us up. It was great to reunite with Juliano after not seeing him for three years and to meet his fiancée in person. We stayed with his parents and his brother who took very good care of us. They were good people. We checked out the sights that Brasília had to offer, including seeing the Estadio Nacional Mané Garrincha. On the culinary front, we tried different local delicacies including oxtail and *feijoada* (black beans, rice, and meat). The wedding ceremony would be a traditional Catholic wedding held at a church that was on a cliff top. After the ceremony ended, we flooded outside for pictures. It was sunset and produced great imagery of the wedding party with the sun going down over the horizon, the sky a masterpiece of clear blue behind us gradually shifting to yellow and orange hues brilliantly accented by the fluffy clouds that picked up the reds and purples, while the valley spread out far below painted in bright oranges from the red clay and Spanish-style terracotta roofs and the vivid greens of the trees quickly fading into the dusk. After Juliano's wedding in Brazil, it was time to head to the land of Maradona, Messi, and Riquelme two days later. We thanked our wonderful hosts and said our goodbyes to Juliano at the airport and hopped onto the flight to São Paulo where we would be connecting to our flight to Buenos Aires. We began seeing sights of the Argentinian character when we boarded the plane in São Paulo. Argentina's national team in some martial arts sport was on the plane. This one tall fella was carrying his luggage in one hand and in the other hand he had his *yerba mate* gourd, sipping from his *bombilla.* Somehow, he also managed to carry a little *mate* kitbag during all of this. We chuckled to ourselves – the stereotype was true. The Argentinians were addicted to *mate.* We enjoy the drink ourselves, but certainly not to the point of traveling with it as a carry on or taking it in a backpack to enjoy while going up the ski lift as my wife later witnessed from a young, Argentinian skier in Colorado.

We touched down at the Ezeiza International Airport in the Buenos Aires province on June 14, 2022. We walked out to a cool afternoon, still feeling tired from the traveling though our flight only lasted a couple of hours or so. Although we had been south of the equator since we had been Brazil, going farther south, the temperature difference was quite noticeable. It felt like late fall for us. After collecting luggage, we ordered a taxi. We walked out to the taxi with another traveling couple who also ordered one. The guy in charge of handing out the passenger's destination tickets to drivers mixed up ours with the other couple so instead of taking us to our hotel in downtown Buenos Aires, he took us to us to the Palermo neighborhood! After using the little Spanish we knew and the help of our translation app, he took us to our correct hotel.

After checking in to our room and resting a moment, we scoured the online reviews for nearby restaurants before we walked a few doors down to Parrilla Cero5. Meal times in Argentina are quite late, and we were hitting the very beginning of the dinner window despite our evening nap. Just like we did in England on our first night, we had to try Argentina's most famous cuisine so to speak – steaks! This was a traditional restaurant in terms of aesthetics and service, and you could see the charcoal grill where they would cook steaks all day long. We ordered our steaks which came mashed pumpkin, which I have not had before but it complemented the meat quite well. Naturally, we also ordered a liter each of Argentina's most popular *birra*, Quilmes. Quilmes was a former sponsor of Boca Juniors so, as a matter of course, I had to try it. Our dining experience was excellent.

Once our check came, we were shocked at the conversion rate. I understood that Argentina was suffering an economic crisis. One could pay with a credit or debit card which would get you the official conversion rate. However, American dollars were worth much more on street exchanges through unofficial means – this was called the Blue Dollar. The Argentinian government limited the amount of dollars an individual can purchase. This control led to a higher demand that created an underground market at a much higher exchange rate which was almost double the official rate. Since we did not have the opportunity to roam the streets to exchange dollars for pesos due to our late arrival on the day, we paid with a credit card. This meal would have been easily $150 or more in the States at a top-class restaurant. It was roughly $50 in Argentina. Our eyes widened in surprise and bewilderment. I could not believe it. We left our waiter a nice tip and returned to our hotel as we had a big day ahead of us. We were going to do what we came to Argentina for – watch Boca Juniors at La Bombonera.

I slept well the night before despite the upcoming momentous occasion. My wife was up at the crack of dawn to go for a run and explore the area around our hotel. She met me downstairs later in the morning where we had the typical hotel breakfast with a few local additions such as papaya and mango in the fruit selection, *medialunas* (similar, but not exactly the same as a croissant) in the pastry case, a *dulce de leche* option amongst the jams and jellies, and of course *yerba mate* next to the Earl Gray and breakfast blend tea bags. Sufficiently caffeinated and with full bellies, we ventured out to explore the city. We first roamed the streets of downtown Buenos Aires with no real goal except to see the city and familiarize ourselves with what was near our home base. What I found interesting about the architecture is that the city looked very European. If someone had dropped me off in the middle of the city, I could have easily confused it for London, Paris, or Madrid. Walking down Calle Florida (Florida Street), we heard "Cambio! Cambio!" This was the call that identified the underground market for currency exchange. If you wanted local currency in exchange for US Dollars at the Blue Dollar rate, these were the people you would approach. So, we did. Of course, we were nervous as it was the first time and the whole thing seemed seedy, so we decided to only take a small amount of cash to see how this works. Luckily, the Blue Dollar exchange rate was posted on the internet so you would know if you were being taken advantage of or not. This rate fluctuated throughout the day. We approached this middle-aged gentleman in his maroon leather jacket, who led us into a shopping center and to a store 15 meters away from where he was standing. The storefront was glass, but completely painted over or covered with cardboard so no one could see inside. There were no identifying signs, no sales advertisements, no name above the store, and the door was locked. My senses were on high alert as he unlocked the door and ushered us into a tiny office room almost entirely taken up by a large wooden desk. Another middle-aged gentleman sat behind the desk with a calculator and a lockbox, ready to give us Argentinian pesos in exchange for our US Dollars. It was an easy and smooth transaction, and we did not get ripped off. Going to the *cueva* (literally: cave) instead of a more official exchange house was not only convenient, but a bit thrilling as well.

We moved on quickly to buy souvenirs and enjoy the sights and sounds of Buenos Aires. Another shock was the many dogs walking with their owners without a leash and not bothering any other pedestrians or running off. This was a common occurrence and left me dumbfounded as to how these dogs were so disciplined. After trying Mediterranean food in Buenos Aires for lunch, it was time to head back to the hotel to rest and prepare for the match.

As stated before, I became an official international club member in summer of 2020 during the global pandemic. The membership card was supposed to be shipped to the local Boca "consulate." This was essentially an official fan-club. Some way or another, I became associated with the consulate in Los Angeles – all the way across the country from me. One of the perks was free tickets to home matches since international members lived abroad. The president of the consulate, Miri, had been a saint throughout the entire process including initially obtaining the membership card for me and setting up the tickets with the club representative Chelo. Not only that, but also helping us via Chelo to get in touch with a volunteer for the club, Arriana, who was half American half Argentinian and spoke English and Spanish. She was studying for her master's in Buenos Aires and working. After attending a match as an international member, she struck up a conversation with someone who worked for the club who then put her in touch with Chelo. After doing a mini-interview with him, she was brought on.

Having an interpreter made things much easier and much more comfortable for us. After messaging back and forth, we were instructed to meet at the Benito Quinquela Martín sports center, which was on the club's property and only a short walk from the stadium. The sports center is named after the famous Argentinian painter who painted scenes of port activity in the Boca neighborhood. I decided to wear my Boca jersey from 2000 with Riquelme's name on the back. 2000 was the year Boca won the Copa Libertadores and then faced and beat Real Madrid in the Intercontinental Cup in Japan. Riquelme was instrumental in both competitions. My significant other wore the 2007 Boca jersey with, you guessed it, Riquelme's name on the back. In 2007, Riquelme returned to the club after his spell in Europe and led the team to another Libertadores title. It was appropriate that we wore Riquelme kits, the club's biggest icon. After we were dropped off by our rideshare, while approaching the stadium, the streets were already filled with fans over 3 hours before kick-off. The driver dropped us off as close as he could with the festivities around us going strong. This was on a Wednesday night with kick off at 21:30. I could not believe the atmosphere for a mid-week match.

Quinquela was a hundred steps away from where we were dropped off. We got in contact with Chelo who found us after I sent him a picture of myself. He led us to several other international members from the US, Denmark, Chile, and the Netherlands. A supporter named Nico, who lived in Denmark, but was from Buenos Aires, flew over the pond regularly to attend Boca matches. The two guys from the US were brothers and were part of the Los Angeles consulate. Like Nico, they were also originally from Buenos Aires, but now studied in the us. Arianna arrived shortly after, and we finally met her in person.

Luckily for us, many spoke English, so it made everything run smoothly and we didn't have the awkwardness of not knowing what was going on or feeling left out. We mingled for about an hour and a half before it was time to walk to the stadium. In addition to Chelo, Martín and Gabi were coordinators for our group's match. We were handed our tickets and began our short trek to the stadium with Gabi leading the line. With every step I took, my heartbeats were increasing, the eager anticipation was building more and more. We turned the corner onto a curved street. Once we made the curve, there it was, La Bombonera, in all its glory. I made it to my Mecca, my Rome. The enormity of the stadium with its great beams and columns from the outside was a sight to behold, with all of it painted in the club's blue and gold colors. I took the moment all in and of course snapped some photos and selfies to help me remember this moment forever.

After we made it past security, we started walking up the stairs to find our seats. I assumed we would be near the top of the stadium due to prior information given to us. But the club surprised us. Due to the small size of our group, the club placed us five rows behind the tunnel where the players would come out. I could not believe it. My mouth was gaping. The experience was already more than I ever expected it to be. Because of the way the stadium is built and our position at the bottom of the lowest section, the terraces and standing areas seemed completely vertical and imposing, adding to the appearance of tightness, closeness, and coziness of the stadium. This architectural build also added to the atmosphere created by the supporters. The architects did us all a favor by not enclosing the stadium with a roof, because I am certain that match would have left us fully deaf if the nonstop singing was given no escape. My ears were ringing as it was. We took many photographs including one of me doing the obligatory pose - Riquelme's famous Topo Gigio celebration. The best way to describe my feelings in this moment would be unadulterated joy. My happiness bubbled up uncontrollably, and I had a big smile plastered on my face all night, continuously turning to beam at my wife as if to say, "this is really happening!" If I could look at myself in that moment, I pictured myself as Diego Simeone sitting on the bench after Atlético Madrid won La Liga on the last day against Barcelona in the 2013/2014 La Liga season. That image of him smiling and laughing after doing the improbable that season always stuck with me.

This was the third matchday of the Liga Profesional. Argentina has an unusual system as it has two separate competitions throughout the year, the Liga Profesional and the

Copa de La Liga Profesional, as compared to, for example, the English Premier League who has one competition to determine the domestic champion for the year. In essence, Argentina splits their domestic season into two separate and distinct competitions. Boca had recently beaten Tigre 3-0 on May 22, 2022, in the final of the Copa de la Liga and hence were crowned champions. This was another competition altogether and had just recently started.

People were filling up the stadium by the minute. La Doce, the name for Boca supporters, but also co-opted by Boca's Barra Brava (which are comparable to ultras in Italy or firms in England) began their chants with their drums, their trumpets, and their voices. The barra brava arrives early and takes over one side of the stadium. Long blue and gold banners unfurled from the top of the stand to the very bottom. A variety of banners hung from all the terraces, with names of players or something else in Boca folklore. La Doce led the entire stadium in song, from kick-off to the very end of the match. They sang for ninety minutes and more and never lost a beat. The atmosphere was passionate, it was electrifying, it was jumping. In fact, it was literally jumping – the concrete structure was bowing dangerously as the supporters all jumped in time. I expected it to be as good as I had seen it on the television, but reality exceeded my expectations. This was above and beyond what I imagined. I was dreaming.

And let me not forget the actual football! The match itself was very entertaining and high scoring. Boca won 5-3. You don't typically get a total of eight goals in a single match. To top it off, goals were scored by my favorite players on the team: Exequiel Zeballos and Darío Benedetto (and Frank Fabra whose shot ended up credited as an own goal because it hit a Tigre player on the way in). The three goals by Tigre were an own goal by Boca and two goals by Mateo Retegui who was on loan at Tigre from Boca. I couldn't believe it. Sitting up close, the speed and pace of the game is much faster than sitting farther away or watching it on the television. One learns to appreciate the game even more from this perspective with how the players must quickly adjust their bodies and positioning and think of the next move they have to make with or without the ball.

After the match, the trophy presentation for last season's championship took place. Apparently, this presentation was supposed to take place at the previous home match, but a lawyer in the club's administration died so it was moved to tonight's match. A big party erupted with the players on the field. The players circled around the field with the trophy while fireworks went off from behind the flat, box-side of the stadium, and cumbia music was blaring over the Bombonera's speakers.

After the festivities were over, we began making our way out of the stadium. Some of our group members at this point left the group and went their separate ways. Since we were not familiar with the area and heard not-so-pleasant things about walking the Boca neighborhood at night, Gabi and Arianna led us out of the stadium, through the streets of *el barrio*, and to a bus station. This walk seemed to last nearly thirty minutes. Once we got to the bus station, Arianna hopped on the bus with us as she was travelling in the same direction and even paid for our fare as the transit required a bus card and we did not have one. We hopped off near our hotel on Suipacha and walked two blocks. It was about 1 AM. We were exhausted. I was also restless but still had some adrenaline rushing through me while I laid in bed with a huge grin on my face for over an hour. I wondered many times, is this real life? One of my dreams had been fulfilled and made into concrete reality. What an unforgettable experience.

The next day, we booked a tour of the city. Our tour guide picked us up at around 10 o'clock in front of our hotel. The guide's name was Facundo, a slender man in his late 40s/early 50s, with gray hair pulled back in a small ponytail. After we got past the initial awkwardness and shallow chit-chat, the conversation moved to substantive topics throughout our four-hour tour of Buenos Aires. It turned out that he was a huge Racing Club supporter and season-ticket holder. I made it known that I was a *hincha de Boca.* We joked about the recent movement of Edwin Cardona from Boca (where he was on loan from Club Tijuana in Mexico) to Racing (again on loan) and his increased frame. He took us to the Plaza de Mayo where we visited the Metropolitan Cathedral of Buenos Aires and laid eyes on Casa Rosada (the "Pink House" – Argentina's equivalent of the White House in the States). Shortly thereafter, he took us to La Boca. We were going to see the neighborhood, where my club was based, but this time in daylight. We began in a little shop where he wanted to explain *yerba mate* to us. We interrupted him out of excitement to tell him that we drank it at home regularly before he continued his speech. He was surprised that we did. He asked us how we knew about this, and we told him we saw Riquelme drink it during Boca matches and wanted to try it out. He then instructed us to walk through El Caminito and take some time to experience and take in the neighborhood.

El Caminito (meaning the Little Way or Little Path) is practically a street museum for La Boca. As you start walking through this part of the *barrio*, you are struck with houses painted in bright, bold colors. The story is that the fishermen and stevedores who lived in the port in the late 19th/early 20th century used leftover paint from ships to colorize their homes. Again, we ran into dogs that were not on leashes but were incredibly well-behaved and even dressed up in jeans or other clothing including Boca Juniors jerseys. As we approached the water, one of the restaurants had two performers dancing the famous tango out front. The tango was invented in Rio de la Plata. Carlos Gardel, the dance's biggest and most popular figure, died prematurely in a plane crash. Further on down, a man dressed up like Diego Maradona would take pictures with tourists for a price. We politely declined the offer. Street vendors were selling small items and crafts. As we made it to the port and walked down the colorfully painted paved-stone street in the famous *barrio*, my fantasy was becoming reality: I was wearing a Boca jersey while walking in the heart of the neighborhood. To add to the excitement, Lo Del Diego, a place across the street from the water, had a life-sized statue of Maradona on its balcony overlooking the street with Diego wearing a Boca jersey, his two watches, and a Fidel Castro style patrol cap with a cigar in his mouth. It was a replica of one of Diego's famous pictures. There were even a few other statues around of Diego and other people of importance in Boca and Argentina, including Lionel Messi. Murals decorated the neighborhood honoring Diego, Román, Martín Palermo, the club itself, and other things associated with Boca (the club *and* neighborhood) and other persons who added to Argentinian culture. We made our way out of El Caminito and met up with

Facundo to continue the tour. He pointed to another building and asked us if we knew who the statues that were on the balcony represented. Diego Armando Maradona (which he knew that we knew), Eva Perón ("Evita" – former First Lady of Argentina and dubbed the spiritual leader of the nation), and the aforementioned Carlos Gardel. "You did your homework, my friends," he said to us. Yes, we did, Facu. Yes, we did.

We got back into Facundo's car. As he was taking us to see the Floralis Genérica, a sculpture that is basically a gigantic mechanical flower that opens with the sunrise and closes as the sun sets in the Plaza de las Naciones Unidas, somehow or another, Maradona came up in the conversation. He told us that as he was driving his car one day, he saw one person sitting on the curb and crying and did not think anything of it. But as he kept driving, he saw more people crying. Finally, he talked to someone, and the news was broken to him that Maradona died.

You always hear of how the football-mad Argentinians deify Maradona. In addition to Diego's otherworldly abilities as a footballer, Maradona was a man of the people. He epitomized the poor and working class of millions and millions of Argentinians. His father worked in a bonemeal factory while his mother was a maid. Maradona had six siblings; he was the first son after four daughters with two more younger brothers born later. The Maradonas lived in Villa Fiorito, a slum in the Buenos

Aires province, right outside the city limits itself. Maradona had to have his wits about him growing up in this area. That would later translate to his trickery, guile, and creativity on the football pitch. Maradona's personality is one that struggles against the odds, the never-say-die attitude, the courage to not back down in the face of difficulties or injustice. As his career progressed, this personality trait was more visible, and he appeared more outspoken. The quarterfinal match against England at the World Cup in 1986 began to cement his status as a national hero. With the English and Argentinians fighting a few years before over the Malvinas in the southern Atlantic and many Argentinian soldiers dying, political undertones existed for the match. Maradona would score the famous "Hand of God" goal and the "Goal of the Century" in the same match, both goals exemplifying his skills and personality. By scoring the first goal with his hand, the deviousness and cunning were on full display. By scoring the second goal, starting from midfield, and going solo all the way through the English defense, his genius, courageousness, and risk-taking were evident. The outcome of the match and Diego's goals were interpreted as revenge against the English for the Malvinas War. Later, in the final against the Germans, he provided the assist for the match-winning goal in the 84th minute. The cementation as a national hero was complete. This had been Maradona's tournament.

I told Facu how we honored Diego on the day he died, which I recounted previously. The emotion shown regarding his death by him was obvious and palpable. I understood finally what Diego meant to the Argentinian people. Reading about it or watching videos and interviews did not cut it for me. This was a personal, human to human interaction that did it. He continued driving us to the rose gardens, one of the more popular green spaces in the city. Even as we pulled into the parking lot, we could still hear a quiet sniffle now and then after the emotional conversation about Maradona.

After enjoying a stroll in the Paseo El Rosedal Garden, it was time to take us back to our hotel. However, a political protest took place in downtown Buenos Aires that was directed at the terrible state of the economy. Facundo could not get through this mass of people with his auto so he left us a few blocks from our hotel. We hugged each other goodbye and farewell. We have kept in touch over the last year or so, usually when Boca plays Racing. He was a genuine guy.

After leaving him, we made it through the swaths of protestors, several of whom were wearing Che Guevera insignia, raising objections to the current state of the government. We ordered carry-out at a restaurant near to the hotel and I had my first *milanesa napolitana*, a breaded fried steak with ham, mozzarella, and tomato sauce on top. You may be excused for thinking that *milanesa napolitana* has its origins in Napoli, Italia but it was actually named after a restaurant in Buenos Aires called "Nápoli." One of the restaurant owners was looking for variation of the original *milanesa*, which was already popular with the locals. After we consumed our mouth-watering food, we made plans for the afternoon to do a tour of La Bombonera with Chelo and Arriana. However, due to the protests in downtown Buenos Aires, no rideshare could get to our hotel and we unfortunately had to cancel. We ended up spending the evening downtown, enjoying the Calixto Bar and a restaurant or two before we called it day.

Early the next morning, my wife ran past the Calixto bar and some of the other bars we hit the night before, and she was amused to see that the last stragglers were just stumbling out of the basement clubs at daybreak, and one or two still had bass notes thumping up through boarded windows and subterranean entryways. Time in South America is just different. After another scrumptious hotel breakfast, the day properly began and we headed back to the stadium to visit the official club store and to do a museum tour. I ended up buying an item or two for myself and something for my buddy Gabi, the producer of the *Boca in English* podcast that had been quite instrumental to me on the road to my Boca fandom. It is the least I could do for him. The self-guided Boca museum tour included examples of the different kits worn since the club's inception, replicas of the dozens and dozens of trophies the club won, imagery of the club's icons with an emphasis on Maradona, and videos involving important moments in the club's history. After we ended the tour, we visited a few unofficial club stores around the stadium and bought more club merchandise. I had to stack up on items; it is not easy or cheap to get Boca merchandise where I live. A taxi picked us up and the rest of the day was spent enjoying nature in the Reserva Ecológica Costanera Sur, a gigantic green space near Puerto Madero in Buenos Aires.

The next day, a Saturday, we spent most of the day doing a vineyard tour with our tour guide, Catalina, at Casa Gamboa, a little over an hour away from Buenos Aires, where we enjoyed their wine and food in the cool Argentinian fall. The Argentinian countryside is quite the juxtaposition to the busy, fast-paced life in the city. There was only one other couple on this tour with us, an English bloke who worked in Brazil and his Brazilian girlfriend. He casually followed Arsenal as rugby was his primary sport. After doing introductions and us telling him that we resided in Alabama, he asked "isn't that the 'Roll Tide' place?" Perhaps Alabama's image has improved in the world. On the way back, Catalina, already knowing at this point I was a Boca fan, told us we were passing River Plate's stadium El Monumental. Instead of looking at it, I kept my eyes looking forward and with a dismissive look on my face said, "that's nice." She laughed and said, "you're a real Boca fan."

In the evening, we were recommended to try El Cuartito ("Little Quarter"), a pizzeria that was founded in 1934. There was a 45-minute line outside of the door and it was worth every second we stood there. The inside of the joint is decorated with sports regalia from various sports including football (representing various leagues around the world), golf, basketball, and even American college football. The recommended item on the menu was the *fugazetta*. It is a pizza that has cheese between two pizza crusts with more cheese on top and onions. The simplicity of it is brilliant and it is absolutely delicious. Of course, this meal was once again complemented by Quilmes.

Our last full day, Sunday, consisted of going to the San Telmo street-market. Several people on our travels had recommended going to it. Merchants lined up in a very long street called Defensa that seemed to go on without an end. Various small arts & crafts, clothes, purses, paintings, and other items were on sale. Once we reached the end of the street market (technically the beginning but it was the end for us since we started from Plaza de Mayo), a local artist was selling his paintings in Plaza Dorrego. We bought one colorful rendition of a couple dancing the tango in La Boca – it was eerily similar to what we actually saw a few days prior. We walked around some more and saw a small gallery that had umbrellas tied together in some fashion near and across the top of the buildings. The various umbrellas were different colors and gave off a cool visual – the perfect tourist selfie spot. Nearby was a central market called Mercado San Telmo. This place was packed with people eating lunch and doing more shopping. On the way back, we bought Boca-themed coasters for drink glasses. Unlike the artist we bought from, this merchant did not speak English and our Spanish was beginner level. So, when he told us the total sum for the coasters, we thought we understood him so we began taking out the money. Turns out, we didn't understand him at all and began giving him more than what it actually cost. This gentleman could have easily ripped us off at this point in the transaction, especially with the current state of the Argentinian economy. However, he did not. He told us to just to give him one bill and that was that. Despite hard times in Argentina, this man stayed honest and dignified in his circumstances. We were thankful for his honesty. We returned to our hotel to rest before continuing our evening plans.

 Boca played away that night to Barracas Central. The area of Barracas was practically next door to La Boca. Since away fans are generally not allowed in Argentina, we watched the match at a bar called Locos X El Fútbol. All the tables eventually filled up and the match was on TV. This is the part where the American tourists play to the stereotype as loud, obnoxious, and clueless. Sitting almost on the other side of the restaurant were these two women with a couple of Argentinian fellas. We could clearly overhear the women's voices speaking with American accents. Their voices were several levels louder than the other patrons in the bar. Everyone else kept their noise level at a minimum, but even across the room we could hear those two. Their behavior added to the cliché of the American tourist, and it wasn't a good look for the rest of American tourists who aren't like them. Despite this unwelcome distraction, we enjoyed Boca winning 3-1 with goals from Sebastián Villa, Pol Fernández, and Changuito Zeballos.

    Upon our return to our hotel, the hard reality hit us that we were leaving the following day, so we began packing. The next day, we had our last hotel breakfast and checked out. The hotel was nice enough to keep our bags for a few more hours as our return flight was not until the late afternoon, and we wanted to squeeze in a few more sights. We walked over to Plaza de Mayo to do some more sightseeing as we were not on such a time crunch as we were on the guided tour. We also returned to the cathedral to look at the artwork and religious artifacts and to benefit from the spiritual peace that the cathedral gave us. While there, we experienced the grenadiers of the Casa Rosada perform the changing of the guard. The changing of the guard is for General Don José de San Martín, national hero and one of the liberators of the country. Our last stop was a tour of the Museo Nacional del Cabildo de Buenos Aires y de la Revolución de Mayo. This is a museum for the May Revolution and the Cabildo (a *cabildo* translates to townhall). It was the city council seat during the colonial era. The building was packed with tourists and space was rather tight, especially walking up the stairs. We ate lunch afterwards at Pertutti next door where I had my last proper Argentinian meal, consisting of the Milanesa Napolitana and Quilmes. We grabbed our bags from the hotel, whose staff was gracious enough to call us a cab, and we headed to Ezeiza International Airport. I enjoyed one last Quilmes for the road at our gate and gave whatever pesos I had left to the workers there as the current was useless in the States. Then it was *chau*, Argentina. We were airborne and returning to the Estados Unidos.

This trip was transformative for me. I fell in love with Argentina, her environment, her culture, and her warm, welcoming, and genuine people. Besides already being a supporter of the national team and Boca Juniors, being in the country allowed me to appreciate what these teams were representing. It added to my fandom and had me incredibly excited for the World Cup in Qatar. My heart and passion were all with Argentina.

CHAPTER 13

Cosmic Justice

Ahora nos volvimos a ilusionar

Now in my mind, the World Cup season with its liturgical colors of sky blue and white unofficially starts when an Italian company called Panini releases their album and stickers for the World Cup. They've been doing so for each World Cup since 1970. You buy packs of random stickers, trying to collect one of every player, team and even stadium. In my part of the world, even finding where to buy stickers is a quest, often facilitated by group texts and social media groups dedicated to posting when a store receives a new shipment. When you find a unique sticker, you then peel off the adhesive backing and carefully stick this player's portrait in the appropriate frame provided in the album. This is a ritual, often done in the utmost secrecy behind locked doors, in desperate hopes that their significant others never find out how much money has been spent on a children's sticker book. The first few packs will go directly into the album, but as you start to acquire duplicates, the next phase of the celebratory season begins – trading. It becomes highly addictive and another way to make friends. I obsessively collected stickers for this World Cup and traded with local friends who also became fans of collecting World Cup stickers in 2018. Once I was done with the 2022 album, I went back and collected older albums from World Cups pre-2018. Why stop with the current edition? Let's collect them all. This served as hors d'oeuvre to get in the mood for the tournament, whetting my appetite and heightening anticipation for the football I craved.

And the main event itself was held in the winter this time around due to the practical impossibility of playing the World Cup in the summer in the sweltering Middle East heat. I thought my emotional involvement peaked with Croatia in 2018, but I was wrong. This World Cup took my emotions to another level. Ever since Argentina's performance in the Copa América, a year and a half prior to the World Cup, I had them pegged as winners. Visiting the country and absolutely falling in love with its culture added to it. And of course, it potentially being Messi's last World Cup and wanting to see him lift the trophy that had eluded him, I was in with both feet supporting the Albiceleste. If I liked Argentina before 2021, I loved them now. There was great chemistry between the players, on the pitch and off. This appeared to be a team that would die trying to win the World Cup for Messi as they had grown up watching him with awe.

For the first match, we woke up at 4 AM to watch Argentina's opener against Saudi Arabia. I made it a superstition to wear different Argentina jerseys for every match they played. It would be Juan Román Riquelme's 2006 World Cup jersey for the opener. And the opener was a shocking loss of 2-1 against Saudi Arabia. I couldn't believe it. After Messi's spot-kick, Argentina were on cruise control but the Saudis scored two goals in 5 minutes. Despite some scoring opportunities, the match ended that way. Were the Argentinians too nervous? Was the pressure too much? Is it all hype? Doubts crept in. I went distraught to work that morning. I saw a friend's wife in her car stopped at the red light while I was crossing the street. She saw me too and mouthed the words "I'm sorry" to me about the loss, knowing my affinity and hype for the South American country.

The next match against Mexico was a must win. I was nervous and anxious watching it in a bar on a day that was preoccupied with a big local rivalry game in college football, Auburn vs. Alabama. My wife and I were like the "Homer Simpson in a bar" meme, surrounded by college football onlookers. A few noticed us watching the match and with typical distaste for the beautiful game dismissively commented on the sport. We ignored the non-believers and glued our eyes to the screen. The match itself remained scoreless after a laboring first half. Was the dream just a dream? It seemed so for a while. The dam needed to be broken soon as time was ticking and in the 64th minute, the water would finally flow. Messi with a low shot from outside of the box to beat Memo Ochoa! It was the goal that Argentina needed, not just for the match, but also mentally for the rest of the tournament. It took care of the psychological crutch and Argentina played much freer now. The burden had been taken off and the water hose had been unkinked. Enzo Fernández would seal the deal in the 87th minute with a beautiful curler. The third group stage match against Poland was again somewhat of a laborious effort but the team scored sooner and calmed the nerves of all supporters with the Polish not giving much resistance at all.

Argentina made it to the round of 16, where they would play Australia. Argentina would be coasting 2-0, but in the last 15 minutes of the match, the Aussies would get lucky with an own goal by Enzo Fernández. The energy of the match shifted, and the lads from down under were seeking the equalizer. In the dying minutes, Emiliano "Dibu" Martínez would make a tremendous save by making himself big and stopping a shot from close range. This was clutch. The ref would blow the whistle soon thereafter and Argentina were onto the next round against the Dutch.

How did my country of residence do and what was my experience with that? The first match was against Wales. Some of my uninitiated colleagues showed a little bit of interest in it so I dragged them to a local bar for the match. Proselytizing to them about the event and the sport was exciting as I liked playing apostle of the most beautiful game to the unconverted. The bar itself was packed with American supporters decked in their colors. The match finished 1-1 with a solid effort by the US. In their second group match, the Americans drew with the mother country England on Black Friday in a match they probably should've won. In a must-win third match against Iran, the US pulled through 1-0 and qualified for the round of 16 against the Netherlands.

We went to a local pub, Draft Picks, to watch the US play the Netherlands early on a Saturday morning. You couldn't breathe in the place. Packed to the rafters, I felt like I was in a can of sardines. When the US scored, delirium hit the joint. Unfortunately, the Dutch were better, and the US lost 3-1. The US didn't necessarily lack the talent to get a victory but had the misfortune of being coached by Gregg Berhalter. He lacked any real experience - coaching for two years in the second division of Swedish football before getting sacked and then coaching

MLS side Columbus Crew. This was boys versus men in the coaching dugout. Berhalter also failed to play Gio Reyna from the start, USA's most technically proficient and creative player. Had the US hired someone who was more qualified and had more serious experience, and wasn't connected to the US soccer establishment, they could've very well beaten the Netherlands. Alas, they did not, and so they suffered the consequences.

The day of the quarter finals that involved Croatia vs. Brazil & Argentina vs. Netherlands proved to be epic. My buddy, my father, and I would eat a hearty American breakfast prior to the Croatia/Brazil match. It was an early rise that day and we scarfed down our waffles and hashbrowns before kick-off. The Croatia/Brazil match finished scoreless in regulation. In overtime, Neymar would play a beautiful pass combination with another teammate and score the goal to put Brazil up. But the Croatians equalized through Bruno Petković with three minutes remaining. We watched with bated breath as the match progressed to a penalty shootout. Our tension found release in shouted praise to the Croatian goalkeeper, Dominik Livaković, who had numerous crucial saves during the match to keep Croatia competitive, including when he stopped Rodrygo from scoring Brazil's first penalty. The Croatians would score all of their penalties and Marquinhos would hit the post on the crucial one, sending Croatia to another World Cup semifinal.

While we were awaiting the Argentina/Netherlands match, we went to get take-away from a local Mexican restaurant called Taqueria Mexico. To me, they had the best Mexican food in town. I was still wearing my Croatia jersey and waiting outside the restaurant when a woman with a Brazilian jersey walked by. She was devastated that Brazil lost. We shook hands as a sign of mutual respect and exchanged a comment or two about the match. Even in defeat, sometimes there is brotherhood.

It was time for kick-off. And, of course, I would switch my jerseys before the match. It was going to be the away kit from Mexico 1986. I couldn't have picked a better one for what became known as the Battle of Lusail. Pre-match, Dutch manager Louis Van Gaal made comments to the press how his team planned on stopping Messi. Dutch goalkeeper Noppert also stated he felt confident in beating Messi from the penalty spot. Messi & Argentina took this personally and did not need further motivation. It would show on the pitch as Argentina would take the lead when Messi threaded the needle to pass the ball through traffic to Nahuel Molina who would slot it past the Dutch keeper. Messi sees openings and spaces on the pitch that most players don't see. The ball passed through 3 or 4 Dutch players. The assist of the tournament for me and one of Messi's greatest in my opinion. The magic man would score a penalty later on to make it 2-0. After he scored, he ran up near to the

Dutch bench, did a little hop, and placed his hands behind his ears and cupped them, directing it at Van Gaal. What did this celebration mean and why was it directed at Van Gaal? To answer that question, it requires going back about two decades and involves Messi's dear friend and the "last 10" Juan Román Riquelme.

On April 8, 2001, Boca Juniors played River Plate in the league. After a penalty was called for Boca, Riquelme stepped up, but the goalkeeper guessed correctly and saved it. However, the ball rebounded and Riquelme ran up to it, heading it into the net. Prior to the match, Mauricio Macri, at the time president of Boca (and future mayor of Buenos Aires and President of Argentina), made comments about Riquelme, which did not sit well with the latter. When Riquelme scored, he performed a small hop, placed his hands behind his ears and cupped them, while implicitly directing the pose at Macri, the point being along the lines of "what do you have to say now?" When asked in a post-match interview about his celebration, Riquelme stated he performed the celebration for his daughter since she was a fan of the cartoon character Topo Gigio, a mouse with large, rounded ears. Fast forward to a few years later, when Riquelme transferred to Barcelona. Van Gaal coached the Catalan outfit in his second stint. Riquelme was not Van Gaal's signing, the latter deeming the transfer political in nature. Van

Gaal rarely played Riquelme and when he did, it was out of his preferred position. Riquelme was not happy.

Coupled with what Van Gaal said about Messi and the team and his treatment of Riquelme decades ago, Messi did not forget. This was Messi's revenge for Román. This was homage to his friend. It was poetic and just.

Unfortunately, Argentina was not on cruise control after being up 2-0. They must learn to suffer to grab a victory. After the second goal, the Dutch changed tactics, brought on Wout Weghorst, and played over the top balls to him and their other taller players. Argentina struggled to control the game. Weghorst flicked a ball with his head in from a cross in the 83rd minute. A set-piece that turned out to be a trick play in the dying minutes of regulation allowed the Netherlands to equalize to make it 2-2. Weghorst was the hero of the second goal as well. It would go to extra time and then on to penalty kicks. Penalties are a nervy business. Who has the better mental fortitude to perform? It turns out it was Argentina, with two huge saves by "Dibu" Martínez to deny the Dutch their first two penalties. Argentina would convert all of theirs, bar one, and the shootout finished 4-3. The physicality and tension during the match, including a bust-up after Leandro Paredes kicked the ball towards the Dutch bench, spilled over into post-match activities. Weghorst wanted to shake Messi's hand after the match, but Messi would have none of it. Weghorst brutally fouled Messi during the match. Messi remembered so while he was in the middle of an interview, Weghorst kept staring at him from a distance. Messi noticed and a famous phrase was born "Qué mirás bobo? Andá Pa'llá", translating to roughly "What are you looking at, fool? Get out of here." Out of the iconic phrase, internet memes were created and so were shirts and other merchandise. It was the cherry on top for a volatile and explosive match. We saw a hybrid of three players through Messi in one match – Messi himself with his performance, Maradona's outspokenness in the bust-up and confrontation in the post-match interview, and Riquelme's rebelliousness in his celebration. In my estimation, they are the Holy Trinity of Argentinian football with Maradona as the father, Messi as the son, and Riquelme as the spirit. Argentina now had a date in the semifinal with Croatia.

Where would my loyalty lie in the semifinal? Ultimately it was with Argentina for reasons I previously mentioned. Croatia already had their moment of getting to the final in 2018 and weren't really expected to perform this go around like they did before. I looked past my ethnic ancestry. The tribalism typically experienced during a World Cup was thrown out of the window. This was potentially seeing Messi win his most desired trophy and perhaps his last chance to do so. Gratefully, my emotions weren't being tugged. It was the least dramatic match for Argentina in the whole tournament. They easily dispatched Croatia 3-0, revenge for Croatia beating them by the same score line in 2018. A sense of calm had come over me through the entire match. I wasn't nervous or edgy. It was a pleasant change from all the tension in the previous matches. Argentina now had the chance to exorcise its demons from the 2014 final, and they would have to do it against the defending champions, France.

"Muchachos ahora nos volvimos a ilusionar." A song that had been sung non-stop from the Argentina supporters, those in attendance, and those watching from far away throughout the whole tournament. It translates to "Boys, we can dream again," referencing the two previous World Cup victories, the soldiers who died in the Malvinas, beating Brazil at the Maracanã and that now they can dream to get the third with Maradona watching from above in support of Messi. It was a catchy tune and the musical zeitgeist for Argentina, its fans, and even the players.

I certainly did not sleep great the night before the final. My nerves were sky high. My remaining unworn jersey, reserved for the final in a display of my supreme confidence in this side, was a replica of the one they would wear on the pitch, with "MESSI" on the back. Lastly, I also made it a ritual to say a little prayer before each match. Football superstitions are part of the game. I was far from the most sacrilegious in this regard – some sisters in Argentina filmed themselves watching the match and praying the rosary.

During the national anthem, you could see it on every Argentinian player's face that they were ready. This was do or die. And they delivered. For about 78 minutes, Argentina dominated the match. The first goal came through Ángel Di María, the man who always comes up clutch in finals for club and country. He tortured Ousmane Dembélé on the wing and drew a penalty which Messi converted. The second goal started out from the back and is most assuredly one of the best, if not the absolute best, team goals ever scored in a World Cup final. A counterattack with quick ball movement and basically one touch passes except for Messi's two-touch to draw a defender, that ended with Mac Allister laying it on a plate for Di María, who shot it past Hugo Lloris. It seemed like Argentina was on cruise control and would finally win the World Cup.

It seemed too easy. Surely France wasn't going to go quietly into the night as defending champions. And then just like in the quarter final and round of 16, the suffering began for Argentina; the suffering to achieve their dream. A clumsy challenge by Otamendi brought down Kolo Muani in the box. Mbappé would step up and convert, even though Dibu Martínez would get a hand on it. The power of the shot by the French superstar was too much. Only 90 seconds later, Mbappé would score a beautiful volley to make it 2-2. The emotional high plummeted to a very emotional low. Would Argentina completely blow this? The match went into extra time. A nice counterattack by Argentina ultimately ended up in the back of the net, courtesy of Messi putting in the rebound after a ferocious shot by Lautaro Martínez which nearly took Lloris's head off. However, in the 118th minute, Gonzalo Montiel blocked a France shot on goal with his arm inside the box and a penalty was awarded to France. Mbappé would complete his hattrick by sending Dibu the wrong way. Mbappé became the second player in history to score a hattrick in a World Cup final, after Englishman Geoff Hurst in 1966.

The French were putting on the pressure and in the last minute before the final whistle, a ball over the top of the Argentinian defense found Kolo Muani who was one on one with Dibu Martínez. I thought this was it. Disappointment. I couldn't watch. I turned my back to the television. Messi's dream and the dream of a nation and supporters everywhere was turning into a nightmare. Messi would not get his hands on the World Cup. The world was cruel and unjust. I was ready to hang my head in despair. My heart stood still. But in perhaps the greatest clutch save in the history of the World Cup, Dibu came out confidently and narrowed the space and angle for Kolo Muani – the latter shot towards the near post but Dibu stuck his leg out which blocked the ball. Cuti Romero quickly headed the ball away and the counter from Argentina began. However, Lautaro Martínez would head the ball wide of the post. What a crazy, exhilarating sequence! It took my breath away. Watching highlights of Kolo Muani's chance to win it for France still scares me to this day. Now, we were going to penalties and getting to the end of this emotional rollercoaster.

The penalties would be shot against a backdrop of the Argentine support. The French would shoot first. Mbappé steps up and converts the first penalty. Messi steps up and converts the first one for Argentina. Coman steps up for France, and Dibu guesses correctly, saving his penalty and does a little dance in celebration. Paulo Dybala courageously shoots it down the middle for Argentina, and Lloris's legs were already out of the way, though just barely. Advantage Argentina. While Tchouaméni was walking up to take the next penalty for France, Dibu, playing his infamous mind games, took the ball and threw it. Tchouaméni had to walk to get the ball again. He steps up and shoots wide of the post. Dibu celebrated yet again in joy as the mind games worked. Leandro Paredes, LP5, the former Boca Juniors player, steps up and converts, although Lloris got a hand on it. The next kick is crucial for France to stay alive. Kolo

Muani, the man who missed his chance to win it for France at the death, steps up and buries it with power almost straight down the middle. And here...we...go, Argentina's chance to win it all. Gonzalo Montiel, former River Plate player, the man who was at fault for causing the second French penalty in extra time, steps up. Takes a deep breath. Runs up. He sends the ball to Lloris's right and Lloris dives left. The ball is in the net. Argentina are world champions! Messi fell to his knees, embraced by Leandro Paredes. The dark cloud over Messi's head disappeared into the Qatari night. The burden that was placed on him by his country, by his supporters, and even his detractors and that he carried all the way to the mountain top, was lifted. The talk that he would never live up to Maradona's reputation with the national team was hushed. The pressure that he placed upon himself was gone. Messi accomplished his final and most desired feat in football. The son of the city of Rosario, the husband of Antonella, the father of Ciro, Mateo, and Thiago, the hero of Argentina – Lionel Andres Messi was finally *free*. He was a world champion. There was a modicum of justice in the world after all. I too fell to my knees, let out a primal scream, and buried my head in the floor out of pure joy. The exhilaration was indescribable. This had been the best World Cup final ever: a match full of drama, storytelling, high quality football, and an emotional journey of highs and lows from start to finish. The fairytale ending happened for Messi, Argentina, and everyone supporting La Pulga and his team. I was still stuck in that moment weeks later.

In celebration, we ended up making traditional empanadas for lunch. Afterwards, we went out for a Fernet and coke, the unofficial drink of Argentina. It was fiesta time! This victory was a long time coming and I loved being caught up in the ecstasy of the moment. To top it all off, during Christmas Day the following week, my wife's grandfather gifted me a little plaque that he painted commemorating Argentina's World Cup victory. I was flabbergasted! I mounted the plaque in the football room. The little sanctuary was now complete. I was emotionally exhausted for weeks from the victory but every second, every drop of sweat, every tear, and every heartbeat was worth it.

CHAPTER 14

La Pulga

The Weight

The diminutive Argentinian first came to my attention in 2009 when I began watching Barcelona after Zlatan's transfer to the Catalan club. From the get-go, I knew Messi was special. I continued watching Messi on a weekly basis with Barcelona for years and years after Zlatan had left the club. The fact that he could be the playmaker, the chance creator, the assister, and the goal scorer in a single match made him an incredible player, but doing it on a consistent, week-to-week basis made him otherworldly. His numbers were stratospheric. For him to do these things on the football pitch over such a long period of time is astonishing. And to do so with a fluid and creative style that was aesthetically pleasing to watch was the icing on the cake. His humility, too, was remarkable. In interviews, he never proclaimed himself the greatest and always credited his teammates after a success. Messi was a likeable guy.

He had won numerous Champions League trophies, domestic titles, Club World Cups, and Supercups with Barcelona. However, titles with Argentina's senior side were difficult to obtain. Losses in numerous Copa America tournaments, exits in the early knockout stages at the World Cup in 2010 and 2018, and the heartbreaking loss in the final in 2014 would haunt him.[3] He was supposed to be Maradona's heir to the throne but could never jump over the final hurdle. To some Argentinians, Messi's lack of international trophies with his country was fatal to the argument that he should be held in the same esteem as Maradona. Other Messi detractors, such as Real Madrid fans and Cristiano Ronaldo supporters, would use his lack of international trophies as proof that he could not do it without his Barcelona teammates, and that he was beholden to a certain system at Barcelona which played to his strengths. Whether there was *any* legitimacy to those arguments is another topic, but when Lionel Scaloni took over as coach for Argentina, things began to change. Although Scaloni had only been an assistant to Jorge Sampaoli and briefly a caretaker with Pablo Aimar, the Argentinian Football Association felt confident enough to appoint him as full-fledged coach. Scaloni's first tournament in charge was the 2019 edition of the Copa

---

[3] Although Messi was part of the 2006 World Cup squad, he was not the main protagonist of the team as he was later on in the other competitions I mentioned.

América. Although Argentina finished a disappointing third place and there were calls to sack Scaloni, including by Maradona, AFA extended his contract. There was something brewing there under the surface with a core group of guys in the squad that seemed different than other Argentina squads in the past. A certain camaraderie and brotherhood developed amongst the squad members. Moreover, not only did players like Leandro Paredes, Rodrigo de Paul, Emi Martínez, and Giovani Lo Celso want to play *with* Messi, they wanted to play *for* him.

When the next edition of the Copa America came around, this was evident. You could tell that players other than just Messi or Di María would do their part. Emi Martínez's saves and antics in the penalty shootout against Colombia and Rodrigo de Paul's performance in the final showed that Messi didn't have to carry the burden entirely himself. There was chemistry between him and his teammates and a coach who understood all of this and complemented the chemistry with his tactics and strategy. When the final whistle blew at the Maracanã in the 2021 Copa America final, Messi dropped to his knees, with tears in his eyes, and his teammates immediately came over to embrace him. This was Messi's first trophy for the senior team. The momentum carried on when they beat Italy in the Finalissima and, of course, when Argentina won the World Cup in Qatar.

The reaction during the World Cup and after Argentina won it was interesting. Numerous people who I talked to wanted Argentina to win it because of Messi. The people who I spoke with who do not regularly tune into the sport know at least a small amount about Messi and wanted him to win it. Why? There was something poetic and beautiful about the best player in the world, arguably the greatest of all time, making it to the mountain top after so many hurdles in his way in the past to finally lift the World Cup. It was simply justice. The universe aligned just perfectly for this result. People recognized the cruel injustice that would've happened if one of the greats did not get his hands on the World Cup trophy.

With Messi finally winning his most desired trophy and getting closer to the end of his career, I had to see him perform live before it was too late. Luckily, he signed with Inter Miami and I hoped that I could catch him with his new club and cross off another item off my football bucket list. This would be my second attempt; ten years prior I was at the match when Argentina played without him against Bosnia. My father, my buddy and his father, and I went to Atlanta when they were scheduled to play Inter Miami. However, after arriving the day before the match, the news was that Messi did not travel with the team due to muscular fatigue. Of course, everyone was disappointed. Prior to the match we went and ate in an Argentinian restaurant. One of the restaurant's walls had historical Argentinians painted on it including Maradona. It was nice to have a sliver of the culture that I so enjoyed in Buenos Aires here at this restaurant in Georgia. The *milanesa napolitana* and a fernet with coke brought back wonderful memories. After our meal, it was time to slowly make it to the stadium. For the occasion, I wore my new Argentina kit with the three stars above the badge and my Boca hat. This was my first MLS match and I wasn't expecting much atmosphere-wise from what I've seen on the internet and heard from others who went. The fan culture in the stadium was different. I couldn't help but think of the book "1312: Among the Ultras" by James Montague in the chapter on the MLS supporters' groups, where he states in part: "[I]t has the aesthetics of ultras and a desire to be an anarchic outsider against the system, even if it was still a hyper-corporate environment where every element of the experience was tightly controlled."[4] The atmosphere was not authentic to my eyes and ears. Others will probably disagree with me, but that was my perception of it. On the pitch, the story was a bit better. It was a delight to see World Cup winner

---

[4] 1312: Among the Ultras – A Journey With the World's Most Extreme Fans by James Montague, pg. 308.

and Barcelona legend Sergio Busquets. His movement, spatial awareness, foresight of when to press or when not to press an opposing player, and crisp passing were world class. He was clearly a cut above the rest on the pitch. On the Atlanta side, World Cup winner with Argentina, Thiago Almada also showed his creative skills. The diminutive 10 that transferred over from Vélez Sarsfield in 2022 made a mark on the game. He's a future star to watch for on the Argentinian national team and at the club level. It was indeed a goal-fest with Atlanta winning 5-2. Plenty of goals and entertainment but you could tell the quality of play, on average, wasn't the same as in Europe and South America. There were some Brazilians sitting next to us during the match with Flamengo gear on. They didn't speak English, but the kid tried to make a few comments in Portuguese. Some of the words sounded similar to Spanish so I was able to understand the gist from the little Spanish I knew. Basically, he was commenting on my Boca hat and stated confidently that Boca was going to beat Palmeiras in the semifinals of the Copa Libertadores. A satisfying smile came across my face and I hoped he was right. Before we left to go home the next day, we made a stop in Lawrenceville; we couldn't pass up the opportunity to get to another big Bosnian population hub in the country and to fill our bellies with *ćevapčići*. Although the trip was disappointing because of

Messi's absence, there would hopefully be another opportunity in the future to see him before he hung up his football boots. After all, third time's the charm, right?

CHAPTER 15

El Último Diez

Honor Him

I do not know where I saw Juan Román Riquelme first as a player. Maybe it was a highlight during the 2006 World Cup in Germany. Maybe my acquaintance was not from a highlight reel at all, and I simply heard the name over the years. But when I saw Riquelme sitting in his VP box at La Bombonera on March 7, 2020, when Boca clinched the title on the last day of the season, it is like I had known him as a player since childhood. A legendary aura had surrounded him.

Like his childhood idol, Diego Maradona, Riquelme began his youth career at Argentinos Juniors. In 1996, he moved to Boca Juniors, making his debut for the senior side on 10 November 1996 against Unión de Sante Fe. Riquelme was hailed as another potential heir to Maradona, the new 10, even playing with him at Boca on occasion. During Maradona's last match for Boca against River at El Monumental, Riquelme was his substitution. It was symbolic, like the passing of the torch.

Riquelme's frame, his ability to retain and control the ball, his playmaking ability (which encompasses far more than his ability to assist), the way he moved about the pitch, was reminiscent of the classic 10, an *enganche* ("the hook"). His skills were absolute artistry. It was like watching Mozart on the pitch. His personality, too, was different. He was his own man. He did things his way. He needed the team to be built around him so that he could execute his skills perfectly. When Carlos Bianchi became Boca's coach in 1998, it was a match made in football heaven. The circumstances and the players around Román were just right. Riquelme's first stint at Boca included winning three league titles, back-to-back Copa Libertadores titles, and an Intercontinental Cup against the almighty Real Madrid which included a star-studded line up of Raúl, Figo, Claude Makélélé, Roberto Carlos, and Iker Casillas. Against Real Madrid, Riquelme controlled the midfield and toyed with his opponents at will, etching a memorable performance into football history. He eventually moved to Barcelona in 2002, but manager Louis Van Gaal, who deemed Riquelme a political signing, played him out of position and Riquelme did not shine like he did at Boca. This prompted a move to Villarreal, where Riquelme would eventually take the little, Spanish club dubbed "The Yellow Submarine" to the Champions League semifinals, heights it had never seen before. Unfortunately, his penalty that would have tied the match on aggregate was saved by Arsenal keeper Jens Lehmann. Riquelme then returned to Boca on loan. He would lead Boca to another Copa Libertadores title in 2007, scoring three goals over the course of the two legged final. A hero's return from afar to reclaim what was rightfully his and his club's. Nearing the end of his career, he returned to Argentinos Juniors and helped them win promotion from the second division (Primera B Nacional) back into the first division. In January 2015, he announced his retirement from football. He resurfaced in 2019, as a club legend, where he was on the election ballot as second vice-president with candidate Jorge Amor Ameal to determine the next administration for Boca Juniors. Román's presence on the ballot carried a lot of weight with the voters. A record capacity of Boca Juniors *socios* turned out to vote in the election and the Ameal/Riquelme ticket won. *Bosteros* could rejoice; here would be a man, a club icon, who holds the institution, the club, and its people near and dear to his heart. After the club wandered in the wilderness for several years under a different administration and supporters thought that Boca lost its identity, it was hoped and prayed that Román would restore it to its true nature.

In that capacity as vice-president, he has overseen two league titles, one Copa Argentina, two Copa de la Ligas, and one Supercup. Though he had retired from playing many years before, he had not yet been honored with a testimonial match. That changed on June 25, 2023, one day after he turned 45 years old. The much-anticipated testimonial would be a match between former Boca players against a mixture of players from the past and present Argentinian national team. La Bombonera opened several hours before the match kicked off for perhaps the biggest party of the year for *bosteros* with musical guests as an appetizer before the main attraction. As the sun began to descend, the levels of anxiety and excitement rose. La Doce, Boca's famous *barra brava*, created numerous amazing tifos & banners honoring and praising Román, including the well-known "Topo Gigio" celebration. This was practically an all afternoon and evening event that lasted five to six hours. I immersed myself in the atmosphere at home by making a little *yerba mate* earlier in the day and as the festivities progressed, fernet + coke. Of course, while donning the blue and gold.

The Argentina team consisted of Lionel Messi, Ángel Di María, and former Boca player Leandro Paredes as well as current coach Lionel Scaloni. Messi received a very warm and welcoming reception by the Boca faithful. They appreciated the greatest player in the world, who led Argentina to World Cup glory after 36 years of pain and disappointment. The Boca team included Martín Palermo, Hugo Ibarra, Cata Díaz, Clemente Rodríguez, and of course Riquelme himself. Three managers that Riquelme had played under were present: Jose Pékerman (who coached him for the U-20 Argentina side and for the senior side at the World Cup in 2006), Carlos Bianchi (who coached him at Boca) and Coco Basile (who also coached him at Boca and Argentina). All the stars were present for Román.

The match itself was a fun, exhibitionist spectacle celebrating Riquelme and Argentinian football. To show how much Román means to Boca, La Doce sang "Messi, you have to forgive me, but the greatest in Boca, the greatest is Román." Conversely when Messi scored, for perhaps the first time ever in Boca and La Bombonera history, supporters cheered an opponent scoring a goal against their team. Although Messi grew up as a Newell's Old Boys player and fan, Messi has spoken fondly of Boca in the past and his fondness is arguably influenced by his long friendship with Román. The match itself finished 5-3 in favor of Boca, but the score really did not matter.

After the match, Riquelme gave a speech thanking the fans, his former coaches, and everyone in attendance. Before he turned his attention to thanking Messi, he swapped the jersey that he played in during the match for a new one. The new one revealed the number 10 on the back with Maradona's name above it. This was significant for two reasons: one, the circle came complete – Maradona during his testimonial speech in 2001 took off his kit and revealed one with Román's name on it;

the other reason was that Riquelme and Maradona were not on good terms prior to the World Cup in 2010 – this was akin to a public reconciliation. Turning his attention to Messi and the crowd, he essentially thanked Lionel Messi for participating since Messi had participated a day prior in Rosario for Maxi Rodríguez's testimonial and had not really started his summer vacation yet. Coincidentally, Riquelme and Messi share the same birthday, June 24, and the fans in attendance sang happy birthday to them. Ultimately, he compared Messi with Maradona and said that he does not know whether Messi is above or below Maradona, but that Messi and Maradona are the greatest two players that he had ever seen.

The supporters soaked all this in. I soaked all this in. Although I had only been a Boca fan for less than five years at that point, everything that happened on the pitch, the festivities, the speeches, seeing the legends, did not make me feel like a newer fan. It felt like I had been watching and supporting the club for decades. Boca embodied that prodding feeling of nostalgia that had been with me for all of the years I had abandoned football. The feeling I got from the club was the same feeling I got from watching the highlight reels of the greatest football legends of my childhood, back when football was played differently, when creativity was still allowed, and players weren't told what to do all the time on the pitch by the manager and were allowed to think for themselves, back when there was beauty and magic and not simply mechanization in the game. Riquelme is the epitome of that throwback era to me. Teams were built around him, and when he shined, the team shined. When he was shoehorned into a system at Barcelona under Van Gaal and played out of position, he was not able to showcase the best version of himself. Riquelme's football was pure and unadulterated. It was art. He was a great utilizer of "la pausa" (The Pause), where he had the highest of abilities to bring the match's tempo down and take control of the ball to judge the situation around him. Whether it was a pinpoint through-ball to another teammate, retaining the ball even when surrounded by more than one player, or a simple nutmeg, it was football at its highest heavenly and artistic level. Jorge Valdano, former Argentinian forward, stated this about Román: "If we have to travel from A to B, most of us take the six-lane highway and get there as quickly as possible. Riquelme would choose the winding mountain road, the scenic route which takes him six hours instead of two." Even Argentina's football rivals, Brazil, have recognized Riquelme's genius and his style of play; they hold him in such high regard that many Brazilians named their children after him with various spellings of his last name. The great commentator, wordsmith, and football personality Ray Hudson, who is an immense admirer of Riquelme, has described his style of play as poetry and something that takes your breath away. And I agree with all of the above. Román, to me, is that special of a footballer and he deserves more plaudits than he gets.

If 2022 ended with Argentina winning the World Cup, I hoped that the following 365 days would be complete with Boca winning the Copa Libertadores for the seventh time with Riquelme as the face of the administration. "La Septima", referring to the elusive seventh Copa Libertadores title for the club, had not been achieved in Riquelme's earlier years as vice president. But the campaign in 2023 was different. Boca managed to get to the final, but in each knockout round they beat the opposing team on penalties with heroics from Chiquito Romero every time. They also beat Palmeiras in the semis just like the Brazilian kid in Atlanta had predicted. The final was on November 4, 2023, almost four years since Riquelme became vice president. Boca played Fluminense at the Maracanã stadium in Rio de Janeiro. The month leading up to the final was torture. It seemed like time came to a halt and years passed instead of three or four weeks. Superstitions were rife on social media, especially seeing things in numbers where the result would always be the number seven. It was to be a sign from the football gods that Boca would finally win their first Libertadores in 16 years (1 + 6 = 7). The day finally came. I made fugazetta pizza and invited my football mates over. I decked the den out with a Boca flag and myself with Boca gear. Fernet and coke were readily available. The fugazetta turned out exactly like it was supposed to. I had fulfilled all of my superstitions, and I was certain this was going to be a festive match. We were going to win the long-awaited La Septima. Of course, I was nervous and anxious. The same feeling that I had prior to the 2022 World Cup final reappeared with a vengeance, but I tried to focus on my hopefulness and excitement instead. However, Fluminense took the lead in the 36th minute through Germán Cano. Boca did not play as openly as I expected, and Fluminense had more of the ball. Nonetheless, after what felt like an eternity, Luis Advíncula leveled the score in the 72nd minute and I exploded with angry jubilation. The match went into extra-time. And it was substitute John Kennedy, like an ever watchful sniper looking for an opportunity, who caught the ball at half-volley and shot it past Romero to put up his side. However, he received a second yellow for jumping into the crowd when he celebrated his goal. This meant that Boca was one man up, and they had twenty minutes or so to tie the match and send it to penalties. However, in added time of the first extra time, a scuffle ensued, and Boca's Frank Fabra inexplicably slapped an opposing player. His slap made no sense, and he was red-carded. Boca lost the one-man advantage. Fluminense saw the match out and won the Libertadores for the first time in their history. I was angry at Fabra's actions and so were many other Boca fans. Anger turned to several days of sadness and depression. Boca's "La Septima" was supposed to be the crowning achievement of Riquelme's vice-presidency and confirmation that he and Ameal were the right people to lead the club as elections were scheduled for December, but it was not to be.

Once the election cycle began, Riquelme announced his intention to run for the presidency and Ameal was his choice for the vice-presidency. The opposition would consist of Andrés Ibarra, whose running mate was former Boca president and former president of Argentina, Mauricio Macri. The old feud would rear its head between Macri and Riquelme, who shared antagonistic history when Macri was president of the club and Riquelme played. Javier Milei, who became president of Argentina a month earlier, was also anti-Riquelme. The elections were supposed to take place earlier in December, but the opposition claimed irregularities in the process. After going through the judicial process that also had its own quirks with judges recusing themselves from the case, the elections moved forward and were held on December 17. This was a battle for club identity. And Riquelme won with nearly 65% of the vote. To much of the Boca faithful, Riquelme is seen as a leader, someone that they would go to battle for and pledge their loyalty to because he *is* Boca. He understands the club's values, its culture, its identity, and its history. He is a commander on the front lines, ready to lead his army against whatever comes their way. The Boca faithful chose football purity and romanticism over a businessman being the head of the club and perhaps distorting the club's identity and making it more of a commercial enterprise. They wanted someone who was going to look out for the club and its members instead of losing the essence of the club's identity. Román's quote "to have power is to have the love of the people" rang true. The majority of the people loved him for what he represented. He was what is called *raja* in Bosnian. It is difficult to translate as there is no direct English equivalent, but it means to have humility from being one with a community or group of people, someone who is there when you need help, a standup guy. Argentinian rocker and icon Indio Solari described him as a "neighborhood guy with nobility." Although Boca is not Riquelme, Riquelme is Boca through and through. The football romantic and purist in me unconditionally supported him. Although his first four years weren't perfect, he was miles and miles ahead of the opposition to me. He *was* and *is* dedicated to "keeping Boca, Boca," a club made by the people, for the people, and of the people and for me, my spiritual home.

CONCLUSION

The Final Introspection

Experience

And now, the end is here. What have I found out about myself? What have you found out about me? I am sure there are certain things you've pondered about what's written in this book by this football fanatic.

Firstly, football has strengthened my bond with my family, especially my father. I learned the love of the game from him, whether by watching my first matches at his knee, walking up the steps at the stadium as a child hand in hand, getting a little money to buy Panini stickers, or chatting daily about it. The impact my father had on me when it comes to the sport is immeasurable. This is how we bond with one another. Football has given us positive interactions, kept us close, and realized the finiteness that we have on this earth making each interaction special.

Secondly, one of the questions that probably has come up to other football fanatics who are reading this is about a fundamental tenet of football. It is so fundamental that it is widely accepted without hesitation. That tenet being that one cannot change their football team. Eric Cantona is famously noted as saying: "You can change your wife, politics & religion. But never, never can you change your favorite football team."

I used to believe that quote without questioning it. However, growing older and more experienced in life and refining my tastes and preferences, I *have* questioned it and accepted the fact that one can change their favorite football team (for the right reasons of course). This is why I think so. Dortmund was my first football love. It was also because I lived and experienced the Ruhr region. The realization that the club was also working class came when I was older. When I rekindled my love for BVB in 2013, it was because I was nostalgic. Nostalgic for the 90s, nostalgic living as a carefree refugee kid in Germany. Seeing the team play in person at the Westfalenstadion in April 2019 was a closing chapter. Leaving the stadium after that match, I sort of had this sense that it was over. Any nostalgia that existed was extinguished after that. It was the completion of a childhood dream because I never got to watch BVB play although I lived in the area and I held on to it for years. It was the end. It took years for me to *fully* accept this fact, but I finally did in 2023.

Why Boca Juniors? When I think of pure passion, when I think of what an ideal supporter should be, I think of the *hinchas* of the blue and gold. Their dedication and commitment are second to none. Their working-class roots strike a chord with my upbringing. The club's history is steeped in a never-say-die attitude and the supporters expect a lot from the players that wear the badge of the club. If you play for the *Xeneize*, you must give it your all, week in, week out. The club legends that are Maradona and Riquelme (along with their beautiful style of play, their talent and skills, and their accomplishments) attract me due to their personalities. They did it their way, they stood for their principles (whether I agree with the principles is a separate question), they were their own men who marched to their own tune. I identified with that. I also fell heavily in love with the Argentinian culture during my visit, which for me was the tipping point. Their honesty, passion, easygoingness, hospitality, and cuisine checked all the boxes for me that I value greatly. All my cultural needs were met. I can easily say that Boca has taken my football heart and soul. It is the community that I looked and longed for even though I am in living nearly 5,000 miles away from the club, the *barrio* of La Boca, and the country of Argentina. The search is over for my imagined community. I found it after years and years of looking and yearning for it.

It is natural to grow, develop, and change as a person. It follows that as a person matures, changes, what have you, their tastes, outlook, and interests change. Their outlooks, values, and principles are more refined and easier to identify. To borrow a quote from ancient Greek philosopher Heraclitus, "no man steps in the same river twice for it's not the same river and he's not the same man." The river moves, the sediment moves, the person changes. However, that doesn't necessarily mean we are always pulled in whatever direction the wind pushes us to. The changes in direction of your journey are because you are looking for yourself, probing things to discover a physical manifestation of your values and principles. As Socrates stated, education is remembering. Education does not have to refer to formal schooling. It can be remembering, finding, discovering and learning about yourself, your principles, your values, and so forth. By having "found" your values, you look for it in its physical manifestation. This for me is Boca, my spiritual home. I can proudly and confidently self-identify as a *bostero*.

Football has connected me through time and history. Looking through the football lens, I discovered my birth country's past with the aid of football. It has aided me in tough times. The beautiful game has helped me in finding my people. It has opened the door for me to the rest of the world. Football piqued my interest to learn about and experience different cultures and their histories. It has taken me to numerous continents, countries, cities, towns, and exposed me to their respective languages, mores and folkways. The language of football itself has connected me with people of different backgrounds and nationalities. Our lives, personalities, and cultures may be different, but the beautiful game breaks the ice and allows us to form friendships. It has made my identity clearer to me and simultaneously made me more cosmopolitan while also more parochial with Boca. It has aided me in personal development. Importantly, it has helped me shake off that feeling of a constant outsider or loner, whether that was finding a community or building friendships. Football has done a lot for me and continues to do so. May the beautiful game live on forever.

ACKNOWLEDGMENTS

Thank You

I want to thank the English for inventing the modern version of the beautiful game and for standardizing the rules to it. You gave the world the blueprint to make people like me happy.

I want to thank all the footballers who I have derived pleasure from watching or who have inspired me over the years, from when I was a small child to a grown man: Andreas Möller, Giovane Élber, Ulf Kirsten, Andrés Iniesta, Xavi Hernández, David Villa, Dimitri Payet, but most importantly Ronaldo Luis Nazario De Lima ("R9"), Zlatan Ibrahimović, and the Holy Trinity of Argentinian football Lionel Andres Messi, Diego Armando Maradona, and Juan Román Riquelme.

I want to thank all my friends who have continued to keep the football flame alight with their companionship and fellowship and whose company always made watching matches together unforgettable: Ado, Memo, Billy, Denis, Sano, Patrick, Roger, Stephan, Juliano, Gustavo, Siniša, Kyle, all the members of the Causeway Rebellion, and anyone else that I might have missed – you know who you are.

A special thanks to Gabriel Aguero, whose *Boca in English* podcast and friendship fueled my passion for Boca Juniors. I would not be the supporter that I am today without him. Thanks to @elcelebr0 whose postings on Twitter and fanaticism for Juan Román Riquelme and his knowledge made me appreciate Román more than I thought I could. Finishing up the gratitude in the Boca world, I thank all the members of the Los Angeles consulate, especially Miriana Valenzuela. My fellow *bosteros*, you have taken me in with open arms and treated me like I have been a supporter of Boca since birth.

Thanks to Christopher Hylland, whose book *Tears at La Bombonera* served as an inspiration to writing this book, and who, along with Stephen Brandt, Kirsten Schlewitz, Dan Williamson, and Chris Etchingham have helped me by answering my persistent questions about the writing process. Your help and advice helped me stay on the writing path easier than I would have done on my own.

Thank you to Papaw Jimmy for his craftsmanship and artistry in creating football themed décor for my football room. It really enlivens my little sanctuary.

Thank you to the following people for hosting us on our trips: the Fazlić family, the Ibrahimagić family, Ms. Karabeg, Ms. Kirin (Rest in Peace), and the Carneiro family. You were wonderful hosts that welcomed us into your homes without question and treated us like royalty.

Thank you to Joshua whose humor, comedy, and friendship made those long hours washing dishes, bussing tables, and making pizzas much more bearable.

Thank you to Ben for always inquiring about my progress, keeping me accountable and moving forward with writing the book.

My deepest appreciation to Dr. Fishman for waking me up from my robotic lifestyle and instilling in me the discipline and desire to be ambitious. I would not be the person that I am without him.

Hvala to my parents. First, a great deal of gratitude to my mother, whose work ethic, perseverance, and high standards in everything that she did was perhaps the biggest influence on me in my life. And of course, for washing my football kits. An equal amount of gratefulness to my father, who kept me on the straight and narrow path, and who instilled in me a love for the game and whose encyclopedic knowledge of it was passed onto me. I learned from the best about the game. Y'all's encouragement has kept me going. To round out the family appreciation, thanks to my sister, whose support over the years fueled me to chase my dreams.

Thanks to my puppy who kept me good company during the writing of this book and keeps me mentally in place and emotionally calm throughout the day when things get tough.

Thanks to my two nieces, who lighten up my dark days with their sunshine smiles and laughter. Simple things like that make a big difference.

Muchas gracias a Sarah, whose metaphorical kick in the ass finally made me sit down to write this book. Her continuous steadfastness and loving support throughout the process helped me finish it in times of self-doubt. And of course for giving life and color to these words about my life and football fanaticism with her editorial skills.

Not to be forgotten, thanks to everyone who encouraged me throughout the writing process, your words of support helped me every bit along the way.

And lastly, thank you, reader, for purchasing a copy of this book and being interested in this *gringo's* story. Your curiosity and support mean the world to me.

www.ingramcontent.com/pod-product-compliance
Lightning Source LLC
Chambersburg PA
CBHW020245010526
44107CB00002B/109